Other Books by the Author (previously Mary Schroeder)

Jump into Life with James Golden
The Practitioner Handbook, first edition
The Practitioner Handbook, second edition
Engaging Grace: How to use the Power of Co-Creation in Daily Life

# HISTORY OF THE CENTER FOR SPIRITUAL LIVING, REDDING 1971 - 2014

*Empowering individuals to live
an abundant spirit-connected life
through sacred service, community,
and spiritual principles*

REV. MARY E. MITCHELL

iUniverse

HISTORY OF THE CENTER FOR
SPIRITUAL LIVING, REDDING
EMPOWERING INDIVIDUALS TO LIVE AN ABUNDANT
SPIRIT-CONNECTED LIFE THROUGH SACRED SERVICE,
COMMUNITY, AND SPIRITUAL PRINCIPLES

iUniverse books may be ordered through booksellers or by contacting:

iUniverse LLC
1663 Liberty Drive
Bloomington, IN 47403
www.iuniverse.com
1-800-Authors (1-800-288-4677)

Because of the dynamic nature of the Internet, any web addresses or links contained in
this book may have changed since publication and may no longer be valid. The views
expressed in this work are solely those of the author and do not necessarily reflect the
views of the publisher, and the publisher hereby disclaims any responsibility for them.

Any people depicted in stock imagery provided by Thinkstock are models,
and such images are being used for illustrative purposes only.
Certain stock imagery © Thinkstock.

ISBN: 978-1-4917-4187-0 (sc)
ISBN: 978-1-4917-4188-7 (e)

Library of Congress Control Number: 2014913008

Printed in the United States of America.

iUniverse rev. date: 08/18/2014

# DEDICATION

This book is dedicated to:

* those early pioneers who brought the Science of Mind teaching to Redding;

* those members and elders who spent an afternoon with me sharing stories about the church: Bill and Win Siefert, Bruce and Dorothy Johnson, Marilyn and Joe Vondracek, Bob and Dorothy Huntoon, Harry and Frances Bleile, and Rev. Dr. James and Rev. Dr. Andrea Golden;

* and my dear husband, Paul, who patiently supported me through this endeavor.

# TABLE OF CONTENTS

## Appendix

# INTRODUCTION

The history of our Center is full of memories, those special times at family retreats, insights and personal growth in classes, working together to improve the facilities, creating special projects, and sharing life's most poignant moments. Some may remember Church Lady, morning bugle, and retreat families or the joy of an old fashioned barn raising when we constructed the sanctuary. And the hours of laughter and love spent in landscaping, burning brush piles, or painting the labyrinth.

As a community we have celebrated the milestones of life together, both the joys and sorrows. We have delightfully watched the children of our church grow into adulthood and now another generation of children is growing in light and love. And isn't it wonderful that we are blessed to have members of our original church with us today and all the wisdom and love they bring.

In the mid-1990s I interviewed several of our elders about the history of the church, which was quite an enlightening afternoon. Recently it was during the time I spent serving as Interim Co-Pastor / Administrator that I went through every box and file I could find to piece together the rest of the story. What follows contains many people, places, and events that you may not remember, but it paints a rich picture of this vibrant community that holds such a special place in our hearts.

A heart-felt THANK YOU to Larry Watters who sorted through boxes of old photos and scanned each one for this book and dozens more soon to be posted on the web site. My DEEP GRATITUDE to Dianne

Brown who not only edited the manuscript for typos and grammar, but shook out the dust leaving a more lively refreshing narrative.

May you enjoy this special look at the history of our spiritual family!

Rev. Mary E. Mitchell

# HISTORY OF THE CENTER FOR SPIRITUAL LIVING, REDDING

## 1971

George and Marge Brenner and Linda Long started a Science of Mind study group in the Brenner's home in Redding, California, and eventually moved it to a room in the Convention Center, followed by a move to a senior citizen's hall. When the Brenners moved out of the area, they turned over the group to Harry (a retired PG&E Pit River Dam financial manager) and Edwina Magill to continue the meetings.

When Harry decided to stop running the organization, they hired Rev. Frances Laird from United Church of Religious Science (UCRS), and she conducted meetings at the Masonic Hall on Lake Boulevard. Rev. Laird had a "Good 5" radio program every Sunday morning, and her treatments were very well done and effective, but it wasn't long before problems arose. Rev. Laird's lectures on Sunday got shorter and shorter, and the number of songs increased until one Sunday she gave a 5-minute lecture. Bruce Johnson and Bob Huntoon were on the Board of Trustees at the time. There were more problems and board members talked with Rev. Frances about it, but she felt there was no need to change her methods. Bob wrote a letter asking for her resignation and she refused, so the board resigned en masse. The next night the ex-board held the first organizational meeting of the new study group at the Redwood Mobile Home Park in the Penthouse meeting room.

The new group hired new ministers, Rev. Hal and Rev. Rosaline Hockett of UCRS. The Hocketts held services in a building on Bechelli Lane, across from Bartell's Burgers by the bowling shop. Doris Payne bought a piano and took care of providing the music. Religious Science International (RSI) provided songbooks. Joe Vondrachek purchased 100 chairs with blue vinyl covers, and for a donation of $10 - $12 you could get your name engraved on a small brass nameplate fixed to the top of the chair.

## 1976

By September 26, 1976, the group was meeting in the Women's Improvement Club on West Street. The next move was on October 3, with twenty metaphysicians meeting at the Ponderosa Inn for what would become the Redding Science of Mind Center Society. Bob Huntoon was the temporary leader, and Dr. Hewitt from Sacramento was the first speaker. At the second organization meeting, Ken Miller was named President.

During this time, the UCRS kept meeting on Bechelli Lane and little by little those members came over to what would become the Religious Science Church.

## 1977

In January, the group moved to the Redding Women's Club. In February, the group collected 40 signatures and applied to RSI to be established as an RSI Society, which was approved. On March 10, Dr. Leo Fishback presented the Society Charter to Edwina and Harry Magill. A society organization could not have a minister, so they were determined to get full church status, which would require 75 members. The group selected a slate of trustees and created bylaws, and a week later decided to start functioning as a church and elected a formal Board of Trustees.

On February 9, the Record Searchlight newspaper ran a great article entitled, "Seeing Oneness with the Creator," which read:

F.H. "Harry" Magill, leader of the Redding Science of Mind Center Society, believes in the perfection of mankind. "I try to help the society's members understand their spiritual perfection," he said. "Perfection is realized when one recognizes oneness with the Creator. There is only one mind, and everyone shares that mind—the mind of God."

The Redding Science of Mind Center is not a church, but a "Society," according to Magill. It began October 1, at the Women's Improvement Club on West Street. "We don't have a pastor yet, but we are working on it," Magill said. "We have contacted the Religious Science International Headquarters, and they're helping us in our search. We expect to have a pastor in about six months."

**F.H. "HARRY" MAGILL**
**"There is only one mind"**

In the meantime, Magill takes the pulpit for the Society's 50 members. He and his wife Edwina are "practitioners," licensed by the headquarters in Filmore to give "treatments for the betterment of their fellow men."

"Our treatments are not the kind given by medical doctors," Magill said. "We believe that thoughts cause sickness and other problems. By applying truth, especially the truth of perfection, we may overcome untruth and abolish mankind's sickness. Magill says the congregation does believe in going to doctors, "We'll accept help wherever we can find it," he said.

Magill and his wife enjoy traveling and are particularly interested in the Navajo Indian territory of the Southwest. "The Navajo philosophy is quite similar to ours," he said. "Their beliefs are metaphysical, the same as our own. But then, similar abstract thoughts are found in nearly all sacred writings throughout the ages."

Among Magill's hobbies is collecting Indian jewelry, especially turquoise pieces. He wears a belt buckle and a watch decorated with the stones. "I enjoy the craftsmanship of the authentic Indian jewelry," he said. "There's so much fake that now the art is no longer appreciated as it should be." Magill also enjoys reading, but says he doesn't have much time for it. "I'm busy right now trying to reform the Society and find a good minister."

"We are a healing and teaching organization that includes services, counseling, healing, prayer therapy, and several classes. That doesn't leave much time for hobbies."

The Redding Science of Mind Center Society conducts Sunday services and Sunday school at 11:00 a.m. at the Women's Center. An advanced Sunday school is offered at 10:00 a.m. with a mid-week service at 7:30 p.m. on Thursdays.

## REV. DR. STEPHEN ZUKOR

In April, when Rev. Dr. Stephen Zukor was named minister, the newspaper ran another article about the Society titled, "Science of Mind goals are right thinking, action." It read:

> After high school in Pennsylvania, Stephen Zukor's choice for a vocation was the ministry. And since that time, the Rev. Zukor has devoted himself to helping others realize that "God is all."

> On June 19 he accepted "the call" to become the first regular minister of the Science of Mind Society in Redding. The society meets weekly at the Redding Women's Club and is affiliated with Religious Science International. Zukor says that the congregation now numbers about 40 members; the number to be constituted as a viable church is 75 members. "That's what we're aiming for right now," he said.

Zukor explained that Science of the Mind is "teaching religion with a main activity of scientific prayer. It's a way of using correct thought for goals desired," Zukor said. "It is based on the idea that Jesus was the 'way shower' in spiritual mind projection. By right thinking and right action an individual comes into his reality," he said. "They realize for the first time the major goals in life: Perfect health, abundant wealth, the capacity of giving and receiving love and creative self-expression."

The religion was founded by Dr. Ernest Holmes who wrote the Science of the Mind text that followers use as a guideline.

Zukor held three degrees in theology and received his Science of Mind training at a church in Redondo Beach, California under the direction of Dr. Frank Richelieu. Dr. Zukor was previously affiliated with the Baptist denomination and preached in churches in Kentucky, South Carolina, and Florida until resigning in 1970.

"I was disillusioned; I knew I hadn't achieved what I was meant for," Zukor said. For seven years after that, he studied other forms of meditation and discipline and found his "closest relationship to God with Science of Mind."

## 1978

**STEPHEN ZUKOR**
God is his all

The Science of Mind Center published the first newsletter in January. Services were at 1407 West Street. Dr. Zukor received the mail at his home at 215 Marina Drive #12, Redding. Bob Huntoon initiated the newsletter and developed its format. Classified ads were accepted to help pay for the postage. The Center had now grown to 75 members.

Also in January, the Center applied to RSI to be recognized as an official church and requested a church charter. The petition was submitted to RSI in Tucson and it was accepted. The name of the church was the **Redding Science of Mind Center** with Dr. Zukor as pastor.

The church Board of Trustees developed ten goals at that time:

> A fulltime operation with church status
> Membership of 100 adults
> Average Sunday attendance of 100
> Move into a building of their own with room to grow as soon as possible
> Establish a newsletter
> Begin accredited classes
> Set up a formal structure
> Set up operating procedures
> Get on a firm financial basis
> Establish children and youth programs

By the congregational meeting in May, membership was 112. The number of seats on the Board was increased from seven to nine members.

The Executive Committee of the Board was formed. The first donation of $100 was received to start a new building fund.

The Board of Trustees included:
>     Don Churchill, President
>     Bill Seiffert, Vice President
>     Alice Scarbrough, Secretary
>     Jenny Pursell, Treasurer
>     Colleen Arendall
>     Billie Sue Dethelfs
>     Ed Ewing
>     Marlene Herrin

Church Staff included:
>     Rev, Harry Magill, Manager
>     Colleen Arendall, Administration
>     Alice Scarbrough, Awareness Editor
>     Lillian Jensen, Transportation
>     Bill Seiffert, Head Usher
>     Margaret Walker, Bookstore

All bills were presented to the Board each month for approval before payment. Each meeting the Treasurer presented a quick summary report of the financials. In May, the Board requested full financial reports be presented every quarter. Dr. Zukor suggested that the bylaws be amended to the effect that certain funds designated for special use cannot be used for any other purpose without a majority vote of the membership.

For the future, the Board saw solid, sustained growth and envisioned a school and holistic hospital. The group received the Religious Science Church Charter #152 on February 3, 1978. Dr. Robert Bitzer signed the charter.

The new newsletter editor was Candace Reid. The March newsletter announced the church charter would be officially presented on March 5, with Dr. Frank Richelieu of the Redondo Beach Church of Religious Science officiating. The church charter was to be presented by Dr. Lea

Fishbeck, minister of the Glendale Church of Religious Science and a Vice President of the Religious Science International Board of Directors.

The new board was voted in at the congregational meeting:
    Bob Huntoon, President
    Billie Sue Dethlefs, Vice President
    Dorothy Johnson, Secretary
    Marlene Herrin
    Chris Maxwell
    Bill Shearer

Bob Huntoon, Harry Magill, Linda Long, and Edie Magill were practitioners at the time.

The church purchased 10 copies of a new hymnal specifically designed for Religious Science churches to be used by the Music Department. Members then pledged money to purchase additional copies at $4.50 each. As soon as they reached fifty pledged copies, the order was placed. Each hymnal had a bookplate made for the cover to indicate the donor, or if preferred, an inscription was made in memory of someone. The church organist's salary increased to $15 per Sunday.

With his background as a Baptist minister, Dr. Zukor was an excellent minister and counselor. He and his wife had separated, and she lived in Florida with their three daughters and two sons. He became close friends with Bob Huntoon. Dr. Zukor tried to keep the ministry separate from the administration of the church, which worked well since the board was very strong. Dr. Zukor met every Friday with Bob Huntoon to review the operations.

On July 1, 1978 the Record Searchlight was so interested in Dr. Zukor, it ran a half-page article entitled "Science of Mind: We are all co-creators with God." It read:

> "What can be said about the mind that already hasn't been said? According to Dr. Stephen H. Zukor, minister of the Redding Science of Mind Center, people are just beginning to realize

what mental science is all about, thanks to the recent emergence of the "New Thought Movement."

"Zukor, whom Sunday will begin his second year as minister of the local Religious Science International Church, says that—like God and the universe—the potential of the mind is limitless. Zukor says the Science of Mind concept dates as far back as Plotinus, the Roman Neoplatonic philosopher (A.D. 205 – 270), and includes such historical figures as Marcus Aurelius and Ralph Waldo Emerson.

"But, in recent years that mental science has developed, especially on the more liberal West Coast, Zukor says. The science blossomed in the Redding area in the last year and a half. The Science of Mind Center was formed in early 1977 and had 35 members by the time Zukor become its minister a year ago today. It now has 125 members.

"Zukor, at age 58, says he has a new life as a result of mental science. He was born in Scranton, Pennsylvania and received his Bachelor of Arts degree at Georgetown College in Kentucky, his Master's degree in theology and his doctorate of philosophy at the Southern Baptist Seminary in Louisville, Kentucky. "I wrote my doctoral thesis on Sectarian Preaching in the United States," he said.

"Zukor was ordained a Southern Baptist minister in 1944, pastoring large churches in Williamstown, Kentucky, Columbia, South Carolina, and Melbourne, Florida. He says that it was during his nine years at the Melbourne church that he began to have a change in consciousness about dogmatics and human needs, especially in regard to healing. But, it was a course in "Professional Hypnosis for the Ministry" that cemented the change in his life. "It introduced me to the subconscious mind, which I had never considered before. Once I got tuned into the subconscious mind, I haven't been the same since," he said.

"Even while in the Baptist ministry, Zukor says he performed a "lot of fantastic healings," including one where and eight-year-old boy had a rash all over his body. "The parents had to wrap the boy in plastic wrap just to take him out of their home. Doctors said the boy may grow out of it as an adult, or he may have it for the rest of his life. I talked to him about his problem, gave him a hypnotic suggestion, and in two sessions he was cured. It was all in the mind," Zukor said.

"But, his healings created a division in the church, and in 1970, "I took a long sabbatical," as he described his resignation. "I came out West and devoted my time to counseling and study. I went through all of the fields I could: hypnotherapy, transactional analysis, Gestalt, Scientology, EST, and meditation. Then I formed a syncretism of my own for the healing process. That wide field of study broadened my own understanding of how the mind works, and what constitutes healing," he said. It took seven years of study from 1970 to 1977 for Zukor to feel he was ready to become a Religious Science International minister. That was when he came to Redding.

"I am very happy living in Redding, and I am very happy with what I am doing now," he said. Through his experiences, Zukor says, "I've come to the discovery that there are three syndromes which inhibit the happiness of most of humanity:

1) The "walking zombie syndrome": in which the subliminal mind is highly preoccupied with death ideas, and since these death thoughts are not know to the subject, they keep on attracting more death-dealing circumstances.
2) "Ponce de Leon syndrome": where one gets an intense longing for youth and has a feeling that life is passing by. The problem is that they become afraid of the adult world through the tyranny of parents, teachers, or older children. A person with this syndrome looks younger than they are, but they are very touchy about being rejected.
3) The "Adam and Eve syndrome": where a person believes they are guilty. They have decided they've done wrong, so

the subconscious finds a punishment, and it is usually a painful process, such as migraines, pains in certain areas of the body, or diseased organs or systems in the body. It is the assumption of guilt and the resultant punishment in terms of pain, and it persists until the mental cause is known, which is usually a conflicting idea or incomplete relationship or unfinished communication.

"Zukor says that what is needed in the first two syndromes is the emancipation of the self so that each one can live his own God-presence with a clear mind. Every human being owes to society an individual 100 percent alive and 100 percent mature, paving the way for you to realize your creative potential and make your contributions to life.

"He went on to say, "We are all co-creators with God. All causation is mental, and we live in a sea of intelligence. The whole universe is a sea in intelligence, and every human being is the center of that intelligence. Thus, the Creator is always creating by means of each person at the level of his or her comprehension,

"As a Science of Mind minister, I hold to the principle, to the idea, the allness of God expressing through all creation. The original truth is that God made man in His image and likeness, and once that becomes assumed and believed as the starting point for all thinking, it leads to the finest in human expression.

"Every human life is an eternal idea, ever expanding. It means life can never conceive of death because God is life. Life is perfect just the way it is. It is the level of our mentality that creates the conditions for limitations, lack, sickness, and disease. I believe in the eternal oneness of God and man. Separation, good, and bad is a devastating thought. To believe in the redemption plan is to believe in sin, and that means separation.

"The first thing to realize is that we live in a universe that looks physical but is spiritual, and this universe is the body of

God because God created it. Therefore, every form in it is a divine expression," he said. The minister adds that sufficiency, wholeness, and completeness are three vital keys to mental science perfection. "That is our faith for all things," he said.

# 1979

Dr. Frank Richelieu notified Dr. Zukor that the approval for Rev. Harry Magill's minster license came in February. The Board agreed to pay Rev. Harry $100 per month as Assistant Minister.

The current lease at the Festebord Restaurant was $160/month but increased to $300/month on a month-to-month lease. By setting back the time for Sunday service by one hour assured that there was no conflict with the Festebord's noontime customers and parking space.

A new volunteer group was formed, called Single Minded, and one of their first decisions was to organize a transportation service for the church.

There was discussion about finding children and youth teachers, cutting back on the nursery, and how best to teach principles to the youth.

At the annual congregational meeting, the two retiring Board members were Chris Maxwell and Dorothy Johnson, replaced by Billie Sue Dethlefs and Alice Scarbrough. The Board discussed the idea of having pledge envelopes and a monthly statement of contributions. The bookstore sales were increasing and along with books, 17 meditations tapes were in stock.

A signed and sealed copy of the Articles of Incorporation was received, dated May 11, 1979. On June 19, 1979, the bylaws of the Redding Church of Religious Science were signed by Board members:
Donald Churchill, President
Robert Huntoon, Vice President
Billie Sue Dethlefs
Edward Ewing

> Marlene Herrin
> Harry Magill
> Alice Scarbrough
> William Seiffert
> Rev. Stephen Zukor

In December 1979, the membership list totaled 179. $36,500 was the projected budget revenue for 1979 – 80. The Board worked out how to transfer revenue from events to the General Fund.

Seven LeVelle was contracted to present a one and one-half day "Mind Power/Body Power" program.

In May, there was a special meeting of the Board to discuss the proposed lease between the church and the Festebord Restaurant. The proposal was to lease a 19'x55' block building located behind the Festebord for $550/month and included the use of the banquet room on Sundays. The church would have to pay half of the cost for a new floor in the block building. There were no furnishings in the building at that time. The Board approved signing the lease.

There was an increase from $0.027 to $0.031 for bulk mailing of the newsletter. Volunteers placed "Science of Mind" magazines in libraries in Redding, Red Bluff, Weaverville, Trinity Center, Siskiyou County, Lassen County, as well as Shasta College and College of the Redwoods.

The Board purchased a locked cabinet and calculator for the library/bookstore. A building committee formed in November when the Board agreed to search for land or building for a new home. Bob Huntoon resigned and Colleen Arendall was appointed to fill the remainder of the term. Colleen was also serving as Administrative Assistant.

## 1980

Published in January, the first four-page Awareness Newsletter listed church times: 10:00 a.m. Adult Discussion and 11:00 a.m. service, with a radio program Sunday morning from 8:00 to 8:05 a.m. on KSXO. Church staff included:

> Dr. Zukor, Senior Minister
> Colleen Arendall, Administration
> Lillian Jensen, Transportation
> Alice Scarbrough, Awareness Editor
> Bill Seiffert, Head Usher
> Margaret Walker, Bookstore

The Board of Trustees consisted of:

> Don Churchill, President
> Bill Seiffert, Vice President
> Alice Scarbrough, Secretary
> Jenny Pursell, Treasurer
> Colleen Arendall
> Billie Sue Dethlefs
> Ed Ewing
> Marlene Herrin
> Dr. Stephen Zukor

The February issue of the Awareness Newsletter announced a potluck called the "Fabulous Forefather's Food Festival of Fun and Frolic for the Family" to be held in the Mountain Shadows Mobile Park Recreation Hall on Lake Boulevard.

The Churchill's hosted the Board meetings at their Palo Cedro home. Anderson's Festebord was the site for the first year of RSI classes, while the Monterio Inn on Hilltop Drive was the location for the second year of RSI classes.

The Awareness Newsletter announced a historic step with the purchase of 2.8 acres of land on Oak Mesa Drive near the Mt. Shasta Mall. A personal loan from Ed Ewing made the initial down payment. Board president, Don Churchill, announced a Building Fund thermometer, which was created to measure the progress that was being made to pay off the land.

Sometime after the New Year, Dr. Zukor had a heart attack. Harry Magill said Zukor was clear he could have stayed, but decided it was okay to go versus going through the work needed to get his health back. Dr. Zukor died on February 25, 1980, at the age of 60. He was buried in Melbourne, Florida and the First Baptist Church in Melbourne held his memorial service. Redding church members and a host of friends attended a memorial service held for him at the Shasta Inn.

Years later, Dorothy Johnson reflected on their time with Dr. Zukor. "We feel we were especially fortunate to have had Dr. Zukor with us for a short time. He was a real orator, teacher, and friend. We still listen to the tapes we made from his weekly classes based on the books: *Three Magic Words, Creative Mind and Success, The Story of the Bible: Volumes I, II and III*. And, of course, his many lectures on *The Power of Your Subconscious Mind*. Bruce and I were always delighted to find out, finally, that we had a subconscious mind!"

The March Board meeting earmarked the proceeds from the rummage sale for a Zukor Memorial Building Fund with the intent to name a library, hall, or another portion of the new facility for Dr. Zukor with a plaque for recording the names of the donors.

At the April 12 special meeting of the Board, Dr. Longe of Paradise acted as an advisor to the Board on voting for a new minister. Four candidates were on the ballot. The voting results were:

Wilma and Earl Burtsell of Alhambra, 297
Mr. Bird, 159
Jim Tunis of Santa Barbara, 152
Mr. Marcus, 130

Dr. Longe recommended a one-year contract with Rev. Wilma with a formal review within six months. On April 12, a Letter of Call was sent to Rev. Wilma Burtsell to serve as minister and she was hired on August 23, 1980.

## REV. WILMA BURTSELL

In August 1980, a newspaper article in the Record Searchlight entitled: "Faith Emphasizes Mind Power." It read:

**WILMA BURTSELL**
**"Love your enemies"**

"Five years ago, Wilma Burtsell and her husband visited a Science of Mind Church to purchase some books. There was no service that day, yet Mrs. Burtsell said to her husband, "Earl, this is where we belong. There is a healing presence here." The couple began attending the church in Redondo Beach. A short time later, she decided to enter the ministry, giving up a career in hospital management. "It came in a period of meditation," she said, of her decision to switch fields. "I realized all my life that I was led in that direction. I never listened before."

"Mrs. Burtsell recently became pastor of the Redding Science of Mind Center. The church holds services at 11:00 a.m. each Sunday at the Shasta Inn, 2180 Hilltop Drive. She also teaches an open forum from 10:00 to 10:45 a.m. each Sunday. "We believe all mankind are sons of God," she said. "We believe Jesus is the son of God, but we do not take him as our savior per se."

"Mrs. Burtsell added, "We believe that where you hold your attention is your experience. The power of the word through choices is what you experience. By changing your choices, you change your experiences."

"Science of the Mind beliefs include: the kingdom of heaven is within man and that one experiences it to the degree he becomes conscious of it; the healing of the sick through the power of a universal mind; and the ultimate goal of life is "complete emancipation from all discord of every nature."

"The religion teaches that a universal spirit, God, operates through a universal mind and that people are surrounded by the creative mind, which receives "direct impress from their thoughts and acts upon them." The faith also believes in the direct revelation of truth through the intuitive and spiritual nature of man and that any man may become a revealer of truth who lives in close contact with God.

"The pastor said the key to one's happiness is love: "Love your enemies. You don't have to like what they do, but love the Christ life in each person. We believe that everybody's religion is correct for them," Mrs. Burtsell continued. "We don't go out and recruit or talk against other believers."

"The former Presbyterian said, "I believe that I am totally responsible for myself, for my own progression in eternity. We feel that the soul moves on and you continue to live and grow." She said her faith now takes a metaphysical interpretation of the Bible, rather than a literal one. Ernest Holmes, whose textbook *The Science of Mind*, now used in many of the church's teachings, founded the religion in the 1930s.

"As a pastor, Mrs. Burtsell described her faith as a "workshop religion" with an emphasis on practicing what one has learned. The services include "treatments," which are affirmative prayers. Mrs. Burtsell said, "We teach them to do for themselves, to be dependent on their own divine guidance. God never says no. Affirmative prayer is knowing every need is met." The pastor said first, second, and third-year church classes will begin September 15. Cost is $45 for the first two classes and $200 for the final course. Upon completing the third-year class, one can apply to become a practitioner—one who is qualified to practice spiritual mind healing. "We do not practice laying on of the hands," Mrs. Burtsell said. "We feel that the healing takes place in the mind."

"Her husband will teach the first-year course, and he also takes part in the services. Mrs. Burtsell said her congregation has purchased 2.8 acres of land near the Mt. Shasta Mall, where the church will be built. The congregation totals about 190 members."

The Board sent a letter to Religious Science International requesting Rev. Wilma's husband, Earl, be granted recognition as an unpaid Assistant Minister to be licensed at the same time as Rev. Wilma.

Rev. Wilma completed taping a series of 5-minute talks to be aired on station KSXO in Redding on Sunday mornings for a fee of $12.50 each. They placed an advertisement in the Record Searchlight's annual church directory.

Work began on the details of building a chapel with seating for 250 – 275 for services with parking for 60 – 70 cars. Classrooms and chapel space together would be ~ 4500 sq. ft.

The Board found out that a group of members had prepared a questionnaire to all Church members in an attempt to bring to the Board's attention their dissatisfaction with the current state of the Church. There was dissatisfaction about the Sunday services and requests to have more basic Science of Mind principles presented. Out of 177 members polled, there were 38 responses, 56% negative and 44% positive.

A team led by Dr. Tom Costa, the Burtsells and the Hocketts presented an all-day seminar called "Health, Prosperity, and Relationships."

Bruce Johnson and Alice Scarbrough resigned from the Board. The Board approved using a small building on the Burtsell's property for a classroom and approved the purchase of 24 folding chairs and a table.

# 1981

At the beginning of the year, Rev. Wilma Burtsell was still pastor. She terminated the radio broadcast for lack of response from the greater community. Fred Erickson replaced Bruce Johnson on the board. Board meetings at that time took place in homes. Next, Ed Ewing resigned from the Board.

The Easter Service took place in the bar of the Shasta Inn. Dr. Earlene Castellaw, from Religious Science International, met with the Board regarding complaints she had received about Rev. Wilma often deviating from RSI philosophy. At the annual congregational meeting on April 26, the membership voted to release Rev. Wilma from her duties as pastor. Board members Dave Waterhouse, Pat Gage, and Bill Moore resigned from the Board that same day. Appointed to fill those positions were Emily Hulton, Don Owen, and Carl Roth. Soon after Carl Roth resigned, Bruce Johnson filled the position.

At the May Board meeting, the Board decided to set up committees so the Sunday services would have more organization. The Board asked Fred Erickson to create an Order of Service with the Peace Song at the end of the service. Committees were: Ushers, Greeters, Facilities Development, Awareness Editor, and Post-Service Social Time.

Eventually, the Board interviewed three candidates for the new minister: Rev. Don Burt, who went on to have a wonderful church in Indiana, another person, and Rev. James Golden. At this time, the church was meeting at the Shasta Inn on Hilltop Drive.

## REV. JAMES AND ANDREA GOLDEN

Rev. Jay Scott Neal planted the idea with Rev. James Golden, a newly licensed minister, and his wife Andrea to apply for the pastor position at the church in Redding, but the Goldens wanted to stay in Oregon or Washington. Andrea had her own business and their daughter Katie was ten months old. They were living with Andrea's brother. Their other church opportunities at the time were in Roseburg, Oregon, Atascadero and Orangevale, California. On the way back to Oregon from their first Asilomar Conference in Pacific Grove, California, they looked for the church in Redding, but couldn't find it, although they did decide that they liked Redding.

James came for two interviews with the Board members. Bruce Johnson vividly remembered the first interview, since it took place in the bar at the Shasta Inn. Bob Huntoon recalled that the only place to meet at the Shasta Inn was the bar, and when they sank into the deep comfort of the lounge chairs, they told James to "have at it" just as though that was standard procedure for them. He said that James gulped a time or two and blinked his eyes to think he was on trial for a ministry position in a bar! Bob said that it was so dark he doubted James could see his notes and, in fact, it was difficult for them to even see James. The group did see a very real latent spark, so they invited James back under more favorable circumstances.

In July, the church received a letter from Rev. James stating that he and his family had enjoyed the trip to Redding. He also wrote that if he were chosen to be the new minister, he would be most happy to accept the position. He was scheduled to speak again on August 9, when they held a second interview. After the second interview, the Johnsons took James and Andrea all over town and introduced them to Billie and the Seifferts. The church needed someone with vitality and they felt James had it. They scheduled a congregational vote on August 23. At the congregational meeting, the votes were counted: 28 for James Golden, 11 for James Tunis, two were left blank, and there was one write-in.

James and Andrea decided the minimum income they needed was $1,200 per month. Bruce said that was just what they could afford. The church just completed a big fundraiser to purchase new songbooks, so Bruce asked James if he would use the songbooks. Realizing his refusal could be a deal-breaker, James of course, said, "yes." His response delighted everyone!

On Rev. James' first day on the job, Bruce Johnson went to his house and asked James to sign Harry Magill's minister license renewal form. Harry did not have the criteria required to have a minister's license, but he did speak on Sundays and teach classes. James felt that since he didn't have the requirements, he could not in good faith sign the license. His refusal to sign the renewal caused tension on the board. James meditated on it for a week and called RSI and asked about naming Harry a Minister Emeritus. RSI said that was just fine. The church bought

Harry a plaque and had dinner at C.R. Gibbs Restaurant and everyone was happy. Harry said it was the best thing that could have happened.

Rev. James rented a 500 sq. ft. office next to the United Church of Religious Science on Bechelli Lane.

A September 19, 1981 Record Searchlight newspaper article announced that the new minister of the Redding Science of Mind Center was Rev. James Golden. It read:

**JAMES GOLDEN**
**Science of Mind pastor**

"The Rev. James Golden has become the new pastor of the Redding Science of Mind Center. Golden, 27, is a 1980 graduate of Oregon State University, where he earned a bachelor's degree in religious studies. He and his wife Andrea have a daughter Katie, age two.

"The former Marine said he became interested in "New Thought" religion while in the service. Through Religious Science classes, Golden said, "I was able to discover that I am a wonderful, beautiful person. All I need to do is learn to express it." In addition, the pastor said he learned that God is "personal and is within me and everyone."

"Church doctrine includes: the basic attributes of the universe are love and law and that love is the presence of God or Spirit in all things. "Simply," Golden said, "it is done unto you as you believe, just as Jesus said."

"The denomination believes Jesus was a master teacher, but that He was not God's only son. "We are all sons of God," Golden said. He said that first and second-year Religious Science classes start in October. Cost for each class is $135. Persons wishing more details are asked to contact him. The church meets at 11:00 a.m. each Sunday at the Shasta Inn on Hilltop Drive.

It was not long before the name of the church was changed to "The Redding Church of Religious Science," which continued to meet in the Shasta Inn on Hilltop Drive. The Golden's daughter Cara soon had a sister, Kelly.

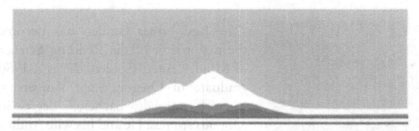

REDDING·CHURCH·OF·RELIGIOUS·SCIENCE

Interior Designer, Nancy Buffum, offered to lease space in her office building next to the Lorenz Hotel on California Street in downtown Redding if the church would remodel it. The Board agreed and the church signed a 3-year lease and moved. The children's church used a room in the Lorenz Hotel. Membership at that time was 170. Cheryl Barnum was the first secretary. Andrea taught her first class on relationships and asked all of the students to bring a gift to the meeting. Contractor Ralph Stearns was in the class and he said his gift was to build a church building.

Andrea received her minister's license during this time, and Rev. Richard Green did the ceremony on a scorching summer day. Rev. Helen Street officiated at the christening for Cara and Kelly.

In September, the Board made an offer on a facility on Canby for $150,000. The church rented additional space at 2665 Bechelli Lane #2 for classroom space. The room size was 20'x30' and needed interior paneling and partitioning. In October, taping Sunday lectures began, with copies made available for the congregation. Rev. Tom Costa from the Palm Desert Church visited and presented the seminar "The Total You."

Rev. James presented plans to the Board to begin a Junior Church and Youth Group. In November, Rev. James and Bob Huntoon presented a draft Policy and Procedures manual. They moved the Treasurer's office paperwork from the home of the Treasurer to the church office so Rev. James could oversee the financials and bookkeeping procedures. Rev. James asked and the Board approved reinstating the procedure to send 10% of Sunday collections to RSI study groups or to new works just getting started.

Don Owen resigned from the Board and Hal Wootton was approved to fill the vacancy. Bruce Johnson resigned from the Board and Vic Panks was approved to fill that vacancy.

The Jack Benny Club was given permission to use the church facilities on the third Friday of each month.

In December, Rev. James was invited to the United Church Board meeting. The United group was dissolving their charter and wanted to transfer all of their assets ($10,000 in value) to the church.

The congregation received a letter announcing the first service of the New Year would be at the 2665 Bechelli Lane address.

## 1982

The Board reactivated the Building and Land Fund. A contract, funded by Joe Vondracek, was signed with radio station KQMS to broadcast a Sunday morning message at 7:35 a.m. by Rev. James. The program lasted about three months. They purchased weekly ads in the Record Searchlight. At first the ads were about the Science of Mind Center, but later changed to Redding Church of Religious Science to better reflect the church organization.

Bill Little of the Monterey Church presented a workshop titled "Spiritual Tools."

Grading on the Oak Mesa property was in process, and the Board applied for a building permit.

The inventory received from the United Church included a duplicating machine and telephone-answering recorder. In April, the membership total was 146. In May, the church scheduled two Sunday services at 9:30 and 11:00 a.m.

The Board reinstated the monthly Board breakfast meetings on the third Tuesday of the month at 6:45 a.m. at the Park Marina Inn. When the Shasta Inn was not available, the Women's Club was rented for $50 per Sunday with a $16.50 per month clean-up fee.

The City of Redding set a public hearing on May 19, regarding Use Permit Application UP-90-82 to construct a 3000 sq. ft. church facility on the property located at 1470 Oak Mesa Drive. Based on the initial study, the City recommended that a negative declaration be adopted for the project, which meant it would not have significant environmental impact to the area. It wasn't long after that the fire department said they would require fire hydrants or a 90,000-gallon storage tank for a sprinkler system in all of the buildings. In addition, it would cost $15,000 to bring in a sewer and $22,000 for water. The board was very concerned about the cost.

The Board discussed the Canby Road property again. The owner came back with a purchase price of $210,000 or cash offer of $160,000, but the building was not quite the ideal size. The property was on a septic system and would cost $3,000 to connect to the city sewer. In addition, curbs and gutters would have to be installed in order to be up to code. The Board agreed to make another offer to the owner of $15,000 down with a purchase price of $140,000 at 11% interest. The offer was rejected. The Board investigated additional options for church property, such as the property next to Big Daddy's Donuts and also a building next to the Carl Jr. restaurant.

The Board voted Fred Erickson to complete Colleen Arendall's term when she resigned her position. The Board also voted Marlene Herrin to complete Carol Whetstone's term after she resigned.

# 1983

The 1983 annual budget was $72,380. Each Board Member received a dove pin with a written Foundation of Spirit treatment as a symbol of commitment to each one's personal growth and to the Church building program.

Article X Section 2 of the bylaws was changed to read: The minister is to always be the leader and director of the church, and shall have the right of final approval of the Board's nominees for the position of President of the Board of Trustees. The Board purchased a recorder and a duplicator to record and duplicate Sunday talks, which were made available for sale.

SHERRY MILLER
"All religions are good"

The Redding Record Searchlight newspaper ran an article about Redding Church of Religious Science member Sherry Miller entitled "There's science to faith."
It read:

"Six years ago, Sherry Miller was deeply impressed by how well a friend handled a difficult period in her life. In fact, she liked what she saw so much, Ms. Miller later decided to become a member of her friend's church that taught Science of the Mind.

"It was a powerful example. As Ms. Miller explained, "she more than coped. She seemed to turn bad things into good things—creative, positive learning experiences." And after attending the Redding

Church of Religious Science, Ms. Miller said she discovered that its teachings were parallel to her own beliefs. "Religious Science is both a philosophy and a faith," she said, adding that the church stresses living life to the fullest by developing one's potential in all areas.

"The Enterprise resident added, "Healthy, happy, prosperous—that's what life is, and I accept that." It was those qualities that drew her to Religious Science. However, she said that the church does not believe in aggressively seeking new members. In fact, just the opposite seems to be the case.

"To me, the big attraction," Ms. Miller said, "was the way other people lived their lives." And that is how her church handles the issue of getting new members: Let your light shine and others will see it. "It's not a church that will knock on doors," Ms. Miller said. "You just about have to find it."

"The church, founded by the late Ernest Holmes, follows the teachings of his book, *The Science of Mind*, *The Bible*, and other materials. Ms. Miller, a real estate broker, said her church also believes in tolerance of all religions. "I think all religions are good and are all going in the same direction," she said. At the same time, there are some basic differences between her church and fundamentalist ones. Her denomination, for example, believes that Jesus was a master teacher, but not God's only son. However, Ms. Miller noted that everyone seeks a relationship with a power greater than themselves, "the common God." Every person is a son of God, according to church doctrine.

Religious Science does not believe in the existence of heaven or hell. "The only hell," Ms. Miller said with a laugh, "is the one people create in their minds."

"The ex-airline stewardess doesn't concern herself about the possibilities of a hereafter. "Life is here," she said, "We have to live life from day to day. The emphasis is on doing the work yourself—and with vigor."

"Besides her real estate business, Ms. Miller is a horse broker and owner of Silky Sally, a thoroughbred/quarter horse, which she rode in hunter-jumper competitions throughout the state. In 1980, Ms. Miller won the high point championship in a show at Lake Shastina. In addition, she's won numerous other championship awards. The Chicago native has been riding horses since her childhood."

The Board considered office space at 3609 Bechelli Lane, Suite F in the Professional Building. Civil engineers submitted bids for architectural drawings and engineering for a new building on the Oak Mesa property. The church still owed $23,294 on the property. They approved funds for grading the property and creating a drainage ditch. A neighbor to the property considered an easement through their property for the proposed sewer line, but it would go through a gully and would be very expensive. They agreed to withdraw their request to pay off the land.

Rev. James proposed a new employment agreement, and the Board approved it. Hal Wooton resigned from the board and Ed Lawson was appointed to complete his term. Billie W. White resigned from the Board and Kathy Hooykaas was voted to complete that term. Joy Johns was in charge of the Junior Church. The Board appointed Sherry Miller to the Board of Trustees.

The Board sent a letter to RSI requesting Rev. James' ordination. Rev. Bill Talifero from Florida, who was Rev. James' teacher when he studied in Oregon, led the ceremony. Rev. Bill would also conduct a seminar on Thursday and preside at the ordination service on Friday.

## 1985

The year began with the church still operating at 1600 California Street. The Board hired Pat Gage to be an Administrative Assistant at a rate of $100/month.

The city communicated that there were no plans to bring water or sewer to the Oak Mesa property, so they decided to put the property up for sale for $35,000 and look at other properties, including a five-acre piece of land on Churn Creek Road. They eventually made an offer on the Churn Creek property. The offer was declined. A second offer was made and also declined.

Rebecca Lowell agreed to create a church sign for the California Street Building.

The Board elected Chris Hooykaas to fill an open spot on the Board of Trustees. Marilyn Wray volunteered to be the church's bookkeeper. In the fall, Andrea was a fourth year ministerial student.

The board began paying soloists $50 to sing on Friendship Sundays. Membership at the time was 169.

In November the Oak Mesa property sale was in escrow.

## 1986

The members liked the variety of musicians that played on Friendship Sundays, so the Board decided to release Blanche from her commitment to play the organ at services in order to encourage other musicians in the community. Andrea worked on a new songbook. The bookstore now had an inventory of $1,825 in books. The bookstore sold tapes of Sunday talks and sales were going very well.

The Board signed a lease extension with Nancy Buffum for the property at 1600 California Street, Suite 200, Redding. The Board opened a Certificate of Deposit at Redding Bank of Commerce for $36,120.85 with the revenue from the sale of the Oak Mesa property. The interest was 8.5% for six months. The Board opened a building fund account at Bank of America. Contractor and member Ralph Stearns volunteered to donate the engineering and draft plans for a new building.

Realtor Sherry Miller found the first segment of the current church property that was two parcels on Hartnell Avenue, just east of Victor. This property was the site for the parking lot and the church building.

Board member and realtor Bob Huntoon did the paperwork for the purchase. No brokerage fees or commissions were paid on the land transaction, since both Bob Huntoon and Sherry Miller were agents. Bob, Sherry, and Rev. James hired Nichols Melburg Architects, and their architect Phil Holcum designed the church.

An article was developed for the Record Searchlight called "Questions and Answers," written by Rev. James.

The Board agreed to use Roberts Rules of Order for their meeting procedure with Hal Muns as parliamentarian.

The Board approved a request for Andrea to be licensed as a teacher by Religious Science International. Andrea also compiled a retreat cookbook that became a big hit.

The Board supported Andrea becoming a licensed minister when the membership reached 300.

The church hired Shar Hofmeister for the position of Choir Director. The first meeting of the Youth Group was in July.

The 1986 Congregational Meeting was on July 27, and Bob Huntoon presented a brief history of the church and a review of the building plans. Bob said that the design of the building was for a village cluster feeling, with a frame and stucco structure, built in two phases, with the first phase being 6,000 sq. ft., and the second phase 1,140 sq. ft. Most of the labor would be volunteers and only skilled labor that the congregation could not provide was to be contracted.

Chris Hooykaas presented an overview of the reasons why it was time to build a church:

1) A building would help to solidify the church and promote growth.
2) It would help center the congregation.
3) The church would become more visible and established in the community.
4) It was time to exercise the group's beliefs in change and growth.

5) The lease on California Street would be up in one year.

The plan received unanimous approval by the congregation, followed by a request to increase pledges to determine if enough funding would be available to cover monthly expenses.

The congregation received a letter sent by the Board on July 31. It announced that enough pledges had been signed to take action to secure the necessary City Use Permits and to finalize the purchase of land on Hartnell upon the granting of the permits. At the September Board meeting, architect Phil Holcomb presented a model of the proposed church building, which had been changed to encompass 8,141 sq. ft., and included a meditation room. The Board approved the final design.

The Board approved selling the church organ at auction.

The new Administrative Assistant, Marilyn Wray would be paid $200 monthly. Marlene Herrin resigned from the Board and Cheryl Anderson was appointed to fill the position.

In November, the Board reviewed a proposal for Architectural Services from Phillip Holcomb based on the model provided for $7,700, based on an hourly rate of $25/hour. The 1987 projected income for the Building Fund was $88,118.

The Youth Group continued to grow with 11 – 13 youth in attendance. Youth Officers were:
>  Joe McGarity, President
>  David Newman, Vice President
>  Kim Williams, Secretary/Treasurer

On December 5, the Board signed an agreement with architect Phillip Holcomb to design the church's new building for a fixed fee of $5,000.

## 1988

The Board appointed Beverly Sorce to the Board of Trustees for the unexpired term of Sherry Miller. Youth Advisors were: Lewanna Eskew and Cheryl Barnum. The Board appointed Lewanna Eskew to complete the unexpired Board term of Kathy Hooykaas. The Board appointed Hunter DeMarais to fill the unexpired term Chuck Hancock. Board president Chris Hooykaas resigned.

The congregational meeting met on March 13. Andrea received her certificate as a Licensed Teacher in the Church of Religious Science.

On June 24, Andrea received her ministerial license at a special ceremony.

The church office on California Street had been broken into twice and instead of putting a lot of money into security at that place, the Executive Committee approved sending a letter to Nancy Buffum with a 30-day notice to cancel the lease. Hunter DeMarais, chairman of the Interim Building Committee, pursued options for office space and location for Sunday Service. It wasn't long before the church rented an office on Hartnell Avenue, moved out of California Street, and held church at various locations for a while. Locations included the Red Lion Inn, Shasta College, and the Senior Citizen's Hall. It was so confusing for members that volunteers stood outside all of the locations each Sunday to direct people where to go. The new Volunteer Coordinator was Jaine Ryder.

During the summer, some building funds had to be used for general fund expenses, which Rev. James followed up with prayer treatment and consciousness raising of the congregation. The Board hired Bob Trask to lead a Board training retreat on June 17, 18, and 19. The Board appointed Pat Keuhne and Sherry Miller to the unexpired positions of Chris Hooykaas and Julia Houser. In August, Hunter DeMarais resigned from the Board.

The church participated in the Holistic Health Fair at the Mt. Shasta Mall.

By November, plans for the new building had been submitted to the City of Redding for their approval. The December newsletter announced completed plans for building a new church in two phases, which the Fire Marshall approved. Phase one included the sanctuary, church offices, bookstore, classroom, and library, as well as the off-site improvements (parking lot, sidewalks, landscaping). The cost for this phase was $566,000. In addition, there was $71,000 in other expenses (loan fees, contingency fund, permits, fees), and balance on the land. The total for Phase One was $637,000. At that date, there was $477,000 available to use toward the construction. This comprised a combination of $92,000 in the building fund, a $270,000 loan from Central Bank, and the donation of $115,000 worth of services form Ralph Stearns of Paragon Development, the contractor for the project. These monies left a balance of $160,000 required before construction could begin.

The Harvest Dinner guest speaker was Dr. Domenic Polifrone from the Hollywood Church of Religious Science.

December 27, Rev. James' weekly TV program, "Principles for Successful Living," began showing on Cable Channel 28 every Tuesday afternoon at 1:00 p.m. and at 8:00 p.m.

## 1989

Many activities brought congregants and friends together in outdoor events during the year. The events included a Cajun Movable Feast or progressive dinner, a raft and kayak trip, and family retreat at Camp Latieze. The camp, which had rustic cabins and a meeting hall was owned by Shasta County Office of Education and was located near Manton. The retreat included meditation, workshops, cooking, with a concurrent program for the children.

*Sue Miller at Camp Latieze*                    *Chris Johnson at Camp*

*Fun at Camp*                    *Workshop at Camp*

*Teens relax at Camp*                    *Odd Games at Camp*

*The Grape Test at Camp*

Permits were obtained, plans drawn, and architectural drawings completed for the new church building. Contractor Ralph Stearns and his crew trained church members in the fine art of cutting a stud squarely, proper nail pounding, putting up walls, and daily site clean-up. Dozens of members and friends participated in putting together the walls and raising the roof, so to speak.

*Construction of the Sanctuary*

*Building under Construction*    *Skeleton Completed*

*Phase One Completed*

# 1990

In February, the congregation made the big move into their new church building, which consisted of the sanctuary, entry, foyer, and restrooms. On Earth Day in April, Awakening Heart Productions presented a multi-media event entitled, "Spirit of Love." The beautiful photography of Mark and Dean Tucker, set to equally beautiful music, created a deep remembrance of our connection with each other and with all life.

It wasn't too long before the 9:00 service started running into the 10:00 service, so in July, the second service was moved forward to start at 10:30 a.m.

*Half Dome Hike for Youth*

The Junior Youth Group spent several months fundraising for their 8-day backpacking trip to Yosemite. Several weekends of local hiking conditioned the kids for the trip and the climb up Half Dome.

*Half Dome Hike*

The congregation celebrated Rev. James' tenth year in ministry with a raucous roast and dance.

*Celebration of Rev James*

Save the Oaks Auction was held to help purchase a land-locked parcel behind the sanctuary that was in danger of being sold to expand the neighboring apartment complex. The Services Auction raised $14,000 and items included:

- a skydiving experience for Rev. Andrea (her first dive and she loved it!), which raised big bucks
- homemade bread by Holly Moore
- bales of oak hay from Joy and Rusty Johns
- a dozen brownies by Dorothy Huntoon
- a Hanukah Fest with Dan and Jaine Howard
- an Italian dinner and hot tub provided by Mark Ibsen
- a bed and breakfast weekend in Santa Cruz by Rosemarie Hill

The StorySingers performed at the church in June. The group was one of New Thought's most popular and inspiring teams who delighted thousands on the West Coast with their sparkling, original music, and unique storytelling style.

A busload of congregants headed north to Medford, Oregon to attend an evening lecture by Ram Dass, a leading proponent of conscious living, service to mankind, and spiritual practice.

Bob Trask presented a workshop, "Common Sense Spirituality." The workshop was a dynamic orchestration of activity, lecture, practice, music, and laughter that assured all participants of a pragmatic and personal adventure.

A delightful murder mystery party was held at Carolyn McHenry's home that included a murder, of course, a séance, and surprise ending. It was talked about afterwards for several years. The youth group served food and beverages. The costumes were just incredible!

*Youth serving the Party*

*The Suspicious Stewart Family*

*Murder Mystery Party Investigation*

## 1991

There was a surprise donation to the church—more property! In December, Mr. John Rodman donated approximately one acre of adjacent land. Phillip Clinger covered the escrow costs, which enabled the church to take possession of the south property. Mr. Rodman had a serious, life-threatening condition, and was not a member of the church, but expressed a desire to contribute something of lasting beauty to the friends, members, and especially the children of the church.

The Board voted to take our "light from under a bushel" and installed a new lighting system to illumine the entry pavilion, sidewalk, and church sign. Live Wire Electric's owner Baron Galocy generously donated much time to make the project cost effective.

The church printed a *1991 Professional Services Directory* brochure. Ads included:
- Hunter DeMarais Business Consulting
- Vesta Unlimited with Vesta Andrews
- Gold Gallery Jewelers by Fran Matthews
- The Growth House Childcare Center by Jaine Ryder
- Newcomers Service by Eileen Weldon
- Zak's Hair Design with Vicki Panuzzi
- Massage Therapy with Brian Cummings & Terri Muse, Stacy Cairns Schnell, Kim Tinker
- Hatha Yoga with Sue Miller
- The Appliance Doctor by Don Duchesneau

Practitioner and Ministerial Student Jeffrey Proctor moved to Redding to study under Rev. James and was also hired as the Administrative Assistant.

# 1992

Tienne Beaulieu presented a special concert, "Windows to the Soul," to benefit construction of a meditation pavilion. The construction fund had accumulated $8,000. As of February, plans for the pavilion continued through the maze of numerous city offices before a final building permit was issued.

Dr. Earlene Castellaw, the RSI Field Service Representative, made a special trip to teach the SOM IV students and see the Redding facilities.

In March, Mary Schroeder published her manuscript of Dr. James' lectures, stories, and deepest insights in a book entitled, *Jump into Life with James Golden*. The church held a champagne book event with much fanfare.

In the fall, Rev. James held a workshop and skydiving adventure called "Halloween Skydive, Trick or Treat." The Junior Youth took a camping trip to Big Lagoon on the coast.

# 1993

The 1993 Services Auction took place to benefit construction of the meditation pavilion. Items included:
* Tai Chi Chuan Lessons by Rae Schlessinger
* fruit trees sprayed by Darrel Rawlings
* eight hours of weeding by Holly Moore
* a romantic moonlight canoe ride for two on Whiskeytown Lake with Dick
* Sorenson and Joanne Pietz

Jaine Ryder-Howard received her minster license at a celebration that also honored her as a new Staff Minister. Jeffrey Proctor received his minster license and left the position of Assistant Minster to accept the Senior Minister position at a church in Knoxville, Tennessee.

Feature Reporter Jon Lewis wrote a wonderful full-page article that ran in the Redding Record Searchlight newspaper about Rev. James and Rev. Andrea and their ministry. The title was, "Golden rule: Couple follows spiritual path." The byline was, "A positive attitude is everything for James and Andrea Golden, ministers who firmly believe that, in life, you reap what you sow."

The article:

*James and Andrea*

"When James Golden, the pastor of the Redding Church of Religious Science, straps on a parachute and jumps out of an airplane, his jump is nothing short of a leap of faith. It is a leap he has made about 100 times in the six years since he took up skydiving, and he uses the experience to illustrate a key point in his Sunday teachings: You have to take charge of your life.

*The Golden Family*

"You put yourself in your own hands, and it is analogous to what we do with our own lives. You have to take charge and if something goes wrong, you have to take care of it. In skydiving, if something goes wrong, you cannot call AAA.

"Developing positive, spiritual attitudes of self-confidence and self-determination are significant parts of the lives of Golden and his wife Andrea, a fellow minister. The attitude has manifested itself in the development of the church.

"When Golden, age 39, received his pastoral assignment in 1981, the Redding Church had approximately 160 members who gathered each Sunday in a Shasta Inn conference room. When those accommodations were not available, the congregation would seek another hotel. "We were bumped up and down Hilltop," Mrs. Golden said with a laugh, recalling the church's early years before it leased a building on California Street next the Lorenz Hotel in 1984. Although happy to have a stationary meeting place, growing membership prompted the Goldens to seek a permanent home. They established a building fund, hired an architect, and purchased property on Hartnell Avenue.

"The big break occurred during a class Mrs. Golden was conducting on relationships. She had asked each participant to bring to class a gift (a poem, song, essay, or anything else that held personal significance), and Ralph Stearns, a former Redding contractor, said that his gift would be to build their church. Stearns donated his services and persuaded his crew to pitch in some of their time on weekends. With a community spirit reminiscent of an old-fashioned barn raising, church members took tools in hand. Working together, the striking 8,000 square foot building took shape and became the church's new home in 1990. "It was a very powerful, very spiritual experience," said Mrs. Golden, who considers the first Sunday service in the church to be among her proudest moments.

"Mrs. Golden, age 36, has another, more recent accomplishment to be proud of: In May, she was nominated in May to be ordained as a minister by the 19-member Board of Directors of Religious Science International, the policy-making body that oversees 130 autonomous churches in America, England, South Africa, Canada, and Jamaica. The Board found that the Redding church, which has 300 members, had a need for a second pastor and that Mrs. Golden had met a variety of requirements, including an appropriate education and a record of meaningful contributions to the church. Her promotion from assistant minister is to be acknowledged in a formal ceremony this fall.

"While the husband-and-wife ministerial team share the same rank, within the church hierarchy Golden is considered pastor of the Redding church. James Golden performs much of the administrative work and leads the services at 9:00 and 10:30 a.m. on Sundays. Mrs. Golden does much of the counseling, operates the Junior, Youth, and outreach programs, and the bookstore. In addition, she organizes annual West Coast youth summer camps for teenage Religious Science church members. "It is all based on self-esteem. We are getting teens to look at their spiritual nature."

"Different paths brought them together and into the church. They met in Tucson, Arizona in the fall of 1975 while attending the University of Arizona. Mutual friends had arranged what amounted to a blind date to see Woody Allen's "Love and Death." They were married four months later in a Christmas Eve service. They have three daughters: Katie, 14, a Parsons

Junior High School student; Cara, 9, and Kelly, 8 are both Mistletoe Elementary School students.

"Golden majored in anthropology while Mrs. Golden worked on a degree in sociology. After three years in Arizona, the couple moved to Ashland, Oregon, where Golden went to work at a restaurant while his wife earned a bachelor's degree in sociology and a minor degree in religious studies from Southern Oregon State College. The couple then moved to Corvallis, where Golden earned a bachelor's degree in religious studies from Oregon State University. The couple settled in Eugene, Oregon, where they lived until 1981, when Golden was called to Redding to lead the church.

"James Theodore Golden was born February 25, 1954, in Philadelphia, Pennsylvania, to Al and Katherine Golden. He attended public schools until the 11th grade, when he dropped out of high school, moved to Tucson, and flashing a streak of independence, joined the Marines. "It took me about 12 hours to figure out I had made a rash decision," Golden said, laughing as he recalled how he had wanted to emulate John Wayne and follow in the footsteps of a close family friend who served as a Marine recruiter. Golden completed his high school education in the service, obtaining a diploma from Adult High School in Camp Lejeune, NC, and went on to serve with distinction, becoming one of only 12 Marines picked to serve as the guard of the American Embassy in Tehran, Iran.

"It was during that duty, with the Shah of Iran in power and Richard Helms serving as the U.S. Ambassador, that Golden said his interest in spiritual matters began. Stationed behind a heavily armored desk in a guardhouse at the embassy entrance, Golden began to consider what would happen if he were called upon to use the weapon at his disposal. "Could I kill somebody? Is it right ethically? I didn't know, but I knew I did not want to kill anybody." Not willing to jeopardize the safety of his fellow Marines or the embassy, Golden went to his commanding officer, expressed his growing doubts, and asked to be relieved of duty. Within 48 hours, he was back in the United States, reassigned as a mail clerk.

"I was all set up to go to Annapolis and become a medical doctor, but I had to follow my spirit," Golden said, describing how his reassignment provided "a real opening for me to look for a deeper meaning of life. I began to look for truth—what's the meaning of the universe? And, the more I learned, the more my interest grew." After the service, he returned to Tucson and enrolled in the university. His parents, who are both retired, live in Tucson.

"Andrea Louise Nelson was born February 2, 1957, in Champaign, Illinois, and grew up in Corvallis, Oregon. Her parents are Robert and Shirley Nelson of Palm Springs. Her father helped build transit systems, including the Bay Area Rapid Transit, the San Diego-Tijuana Trolley, and the Atlanta transit system. For the Atlanta job, Nelson moved his family to Tucker, a suburb of Atlanta. For Andrea, who was still in high school, the transition from the Pacific Northwest to the South was not a smooth one. Exposed to racism, a new culture, and a new climate, she was more than happy to move to Tucson and live with her grandmother after graduating from Tucker High School. "I hated Atlanta," she stated flatly. However, her self-imposed isolation while living in Georgia afforded plenty of time to read, and one book in particular, Aldous Huxley's *Island* become a pivotal point in her spiritual development. "I had always had my own understanding of God. I read *Island* and it was the first I had ever read of someone who felt like I did. I went to Tucson looking for spiritually oriented people," Mrs. Golden said.

"It was in Tucson where the Goldens were first introduced to the Church of Religious Science. "We went right into the church. It dovetailed perfectly with the way we wanted to live our lives," she said. According to Golden, the Church of Religious Science founded in the early 1900s by Dr. Ernest Holmes, holds that all people are inherently spiritual and that God's spirit is expressed through people. "We believe there is one universal truth and that the various religions are wonderful ways of expressing that truth . . . the universal truth is the essential unity between man and God. The spiritual path is to reawaken or discover a unity that already exists."

"The church's teaching, The Science of Mind, holds that a person's thoughts and beliefs create one's reality. "Our thoughts create our own destiny. It is cause and effect: You are the author of your experience," Golden said."

# 1994

Rev. James, now elected to the Religious Science International Board of Directors, became head of the Credentials and Placement Committee.

The Redding Board started a Challenge Fund to complete the exterior of the meditation pavilion. It was not long before the fund met the goals, and the roof and exterior of the pavilion were completed. Larry Taylor of Big Red's BBQ provided a special barbeque to celebrate all of the efforts that were put into creating the cottage and meditation pavilion on the church property.

The RCRS Singles Group, led by Paul Mitchell and Mary Schroeder, enjoyed a weekend retreat in Ashland, Oregon with an evening at the Britt Music Festival. Later on, the group arranged another bus trip back to Oregon to see *Much Ado About Nothing* at the Ashland Shakespeare Theater.

Church Administrator, Charlotte Grom, wed the special man in her life, Ron Schmidt.

The church published a *1994 Services Directory* that included ads from:
- Caretaker Companion by Rosa Zupancic
- Source Biological Pest Control by Beverly Sorce
- Dentist Wayne Crabtree
- Optometrist Kelsey Jewett

- Chiropractor Rick Copeland
- Live Wire Electric with Baran Galocy
- Real Estate Agents Teresa Lavagnino, Larry Whetstone, Hal Delahoussaye, Charlotte Garland
- State Farm Insurance by Sherry Miller
- Tax Preparation with Deb Black
- Visionary Insights by Kristin Idema

In November, a ceremony and celebration honored Rev. James as a Doctor of Religious Science. Rev. Dr. Arleen Bump from Ft. Lauderdale, Florida officiated at the event.

## 1995

Head Start leased the Children's Cottage for their classes during the week.

The church held a Founder's Day Potluck to celebrate the 17th year of the church and the fifth year in the new building.

Dr. James hosted a weekly computer chat on metaphysical topics, called "America On Line." In the fall, Dr. James began a Fourth Year Ministerial Training Class. Students included:
- Alice Carpenter
- J.D. Hunt
- Sharon Kennedy
- Teresa Lavagnino
- Paul Mitchell
- Holly Moore
- Toni Thomas-Niemiec
- Mary Schroeder
- Tresha Wing

The church renewed is Adopt-A-Highway Program on a two-mile stretch of the north-bound lane of I-5 between Knighton Road and the Bonneyview exit.

The church held a special meditation retreat weekend at Camp Latieze in April. It was entitled "Getting Rid of What You Haven't Got!" Over fifty people attended and came home much lighter and happier.

Rev. Andrea was a guest speaker at the Mardi Gras held at the College of the Siskiyous in Weed. The proceeds went to the Fund for Prevention of Siskiyou Domestic Violence.

Member Rev. Sandra Rudh was installed as pastor of the Mt. Shasta Church of Religious Science and the church received charter status. Rev. Jaine Ryder-Howard took the position as pastor of the Contra Costa Church of Religious Science.

Dr. James and Rev. Andrea celebrated their twentieth wedding anniversary.

In 1995, a Services Auction took place with offerings that included:
- a Cioppino dinner for eight by John Sharrah
- rototilling by Ray Garland
- Tahitian dance lessons by Jan Ulrich
- haircuts for Dr. James for a year by hair stylist Vicki Panuzzi
- housecleaning by Dawn Corbin
- homemade Soup for six people monthly for six months by Joe and Toni Niemiec

# 1996

*Meditation Pavilion Construction*

The New Year began with the completion of the Meditation Pavilion. Rev. Joe Niemiec remembers when the pavilion was under construction in the winter, the teachers and "tweens" were so impatient to have their own space they started Sunday mornings out there without heat. The tweens did not like the smell of kerosene, and at that time, no electrical outlets were available for space heaters. Joe was grateful that it was a relatively mild winter. The first mini-meditation retreat took place on January 5 – 6. The church held the next meditation retreat on March 29 – 31. It was entitled "The Heart is the Hub of all Sacred Places."

Gerri Bousseau and Lauri Gibson presented a six-week parenting class, based on the principles of love and logic taught by the Cline-Fay Institute.

New Board members were Paul Mitchell and Carol Chase-Rapin, who replaced Sharon Kennedy and Toni Thomas-Niemiec.

Mary Schroeder resigned from the Board to open up more time to serve on the Board of Religious Science International. The Redding Board appointed Rev. Pam Sanchez to fill her position.

The Chico Church Choir performed at a February service, and the HeartSangha Choir sponsored a potluck for the 45-member troupe. Charlie Thweat returned to present a wonderful concert, "Harmonizing Your Soul."

*Skydiving Adventure*

Rev. James took several members on a skydiving trip the morning after his seminar, "Life is Risky Business." The members carpooled to Davis in time for an introductory class, followed by a tandem skydive from 9,000 feet, with each person securely attached to a professionally trained tandem instructor.

Rev. Jaine Ryder-Howard returned to present a workshop entitled, "Celebration!"

A stained glass memorial fund was initially started to honor Andrea's mother who passed that year. Everyone was invited to participate and a total of 33 donors contributed. The fund fully paid for an exquisite stained glass of oak trees for the window above the podium and side windows. The design was chosen to represent the oak trees that were previously behind the sanctuary that blew down in a storm. On Sundays the congregation could see the

*Stained Glass Memorial*

trees through the window, but also the squirrels scampering around and birds nesting in the trees. Tom Ivicevish was the designer and creator of the magnificent memorial windows that truly captured the hearts of the congregation.

The Board attended a retreat presented by Rich Haggard, a professional board trainer.

Rev. James was accepted as a chaplain for the Redding Police Department and also served on the Chaplaincy Advisory Board at Redding Medical Center.

The Youth Group held an annual talent show and spaghetti feed. The Jr. Youth enjoyed a camping trip on the coast.

The church and folks from the Mt. Shasta Church of Religious Science had a joint picnic lunch in Caldwell Park.

A seven-week series of small Affinity Group discussions were organized for the summer program and included:
- Metaphysical Bible Study
- Writing as a Spiritual Tool
- Life Assessment
- Financial Freedom Forever

Dr. John McMurphy presented a seminar entitled, "Living Deliberately," which combined insights and techniques from Thoreau, Emerson, Filmore, Jung, and Holmes.

Science of Mind ministerial students Sharon Kennedy, Holly Moore, and Toni Thomas-Niemiec presented a workshop called, "Your Adventurous Spirit on Life's Highway."

The first church camping trip to Patrick's Point on the coast took place in June and included community breakfasts, potluck dinners, a campfire talent show, and Sunday outdoor service.

Dr. James and Rev. Andrea held a couple's retreat in Arcata, at a facility nestled in the redwoods.

Science of Mind ministerial students Tresha Wing, Teresa Lavagnino, and Alice Carpenter presented a seminar called, "Savor the Joy in Your Life!" Science of Mind ministerial students J.D. Hunt, Paul Mitchell, and Mary Schroeder presented a seminar, "Choose Prosperity Now!"

A North State Lock-In for Teens took place, which welcomed teens from Fresno to Eugene.

An eight-week summer program, "The Joyful Child," was held for children from ages five to twelve years old. The school hours were 8:00 a.m. to 2:00 p.m. during the week.

The Source Youth Group had 36 teens and six advisors regularly attending weekly group meetings. To get everyone to camp, the group had a Bowl-a-Thon with pledge donations and a special rummage sale.

Church members and friends participated in the Co-Ed Interfaith Softball League with First United Methodist, First Christian, Sacred Heart Catholic, and St. James Lutheran churches.

*Puttin' on the Ritz*

*Medieval Monks*                    *Hawaiian Luau*

"Puttin' on the Ritz" was the theme for the annual Harvest Dinner with music by Lou White and his band. There were dance lessons after Sunday services a few weeks before the party in order to get everyone prepared.

# 1997

In the February newsletter, it noted the church celebrated its 19th year as a chartered Church of Religious Science International. Reflecting on the physical construction of the church during that time, Frances Bleile said, "Within the first five minutes on the first day, someone hit their finger with a hammer, and there was blood everywhere! Dr. James stopped the work, got everyone together, and gave a treatment. He emphasized that we were there to build a church, not to have accidents. From that point on, as far as I know, no one got so much as a scratch. And people were hanging from the rafters—all sorts of dangerous things!" Grace Yung recalled, "I remember Frances Bleile walking around like she was a builder. There was nothing she didn't do. There was nothing anybody didn't do. Everybody was crawling around like they knew what they were doing . . . and when they got it done, it was beautiful! You can't imagine the love and caring that was there. We had a dream, and we were going to do it." Rev. Andrea reflected, "I remember looking up and seeing James and Sandy Scott working way up high on the roof and the rafters. There was a pulley system rigged up, and they would lower a rope and tie up the lengths of wood and haul them up to build the ceiling. There they were, hanging in thin air, nailing those boards." Frances Bleile said, "You know, if anybody falls, all we have to do is throw ourselves to the ground spread eagle, and we'll break their fall—onward and upward to the next phase of building!"

Rev. Carol Chase-Rapin became the new Assistant Minister for the church.

Shasta County Head Start leased the cottage for class during the week, while Children's Church met in the cottage on Sundays.

Rev. Pam Sanchez became the new minister for the Mt. Shasta Society.

Practitioner Kay and Mike Stewart moved to the Bay Area for Mike's job transfer and to be closer to Kay's mother.

Rev. Tresha Wing began the Open Vistas Religious Science Society in Red Bluff.

Dr. James and Rev. Andrea officiated at the ordination of Rev. Jeffrey Proctor in Knoxville, Tennessee in February.

The Gaden Shartse Buddhist Monks visited Redding once again and presented a healing ceremony for the public.

After being presented to the congregation, the new RCRS Endowment Fund offered congregants and friends various methods for planned giving into an account where the principle would never be spent and only interest used each year for special projects to benefit the church. The first step was to build the Endowment Fund up to $50,000 before any interest was spent.

Synaptic Gap, a vocal trio from Rev. Jeffrey Proctor's church in Knoxville, Tennessee traveled cross-country in a van on what they dubbed their

"Tin Can Tour," and presented a great concert. The group shared their unique sound of pop/rock, folk, classical, gospel, and Motown.

The church had a new Meditation Video Production Team, organized by Lynn Fritz, with Paul Mitchell as the Team Leader, Board Member, Mary Schroeder as the scriptwriter, and Mike Stewart as the Technical Advisor. Other team members were: Steve Brooks, Adrienne Cowling, Rich Goates, Rene LaLaberte, Sharon McClure, Sherry Miller, Darrel Rawlings, and Andy Turner. The video featured Dr. James explaining methods of meditation, and the bookstore sold the final product.

The Redding Police Department presented Dr. James with his shield—a metal badge worn by all officers and chaplains. The Department expressed gratitude to the congregation for accepting and supporting Dr. James in his duties as a chaplain. The Children's Church adopted two police officers, Officer Karen Caldwell and Officer Robert Cochran. The kids did prayer treatment for the officers and sent them notes and drawings to express appreciation for their service.

Andrea received her minister license and Dr. James presented the new Reverend with a gift of a Caribbean Wind Jammer Adventure in the Wind Islands off South America.

The church began selling some of the old stackable, blue vinyl chairs with grey metal frames for $10 each.

Congregants attended the musical play, "Godspell," at the Phoenix Theater to celebrate member Debbie Barnes, who had one of the lead roles.

Jonathan Young, Ph.D. and curator of the Joseph Campbell Archives & Library presented a seminar, "Finding Your Way Back Home."

# 1998

Early in the New Year, the church expansion loan and construction of a new wing were delayed because of problems with completing the required architectural services. The architect was unable to fulfill the terms of his contract, so the board solicited new proposals for the work.

In February, the church celebrated its 20th anniversary with birthday cake enjoyed by all.

Under the leadership of Leslie Finch, members continued participating in the Adopt-A-Highway Program, picking up trash periodically along the length of Interstate 5, from the Knighton Road to Bonneyview Road exits.

Rev. Carol Chase-Rapin organized a cross-country ski trip and seminar, "From Fear to Power," and skiing instructions were given by Don Duscheneau and Larry Moore.

In spring there was a wedding vow renewal ceremony and everyone enjoyed celebrating the longest married couple that participated, Harry and Francis Bleile.

## REDDING CHURCH of RELIGIOUS SCIENCE

The Church of Religious Science adopted a new logo with a spray of oak branches and leaves over the title.

A local Alcoholics Anonymous group began to meet in the Social Hall on Tuesdays from 5:30 to 6:30 p. m.

Singer Charley Thweatt came to present a workshop, "The Power of a Focused Heart," and a concert, "I Am Spirit."

Practitioner Sharon Kennedy received the most precious gift, a healthy kidney from her husband. It was a blessed miracle of life!

The church offered a three and one half day wilderness orienteering solo course in the wilderness area around Mt. Shasta for ten participants. Dr. James, Rev. Andrea, Dan and Lorre Rizzi, and Chris and Kathy Hooykaas provide their combined knowledge of camping and wilderness adventures for the brave souls sent into the wilds.

*Wilderness Adventure: James And Sue*

Swami Beyondananda, aka Steve Bhaerman, presented an inspirational performance, "Duck Soup for the Soul."

A 1998 Services Auction included:
- an East Indian Dinner for six by Kathleen Breslin and Helen Peterson
- homemade desert of the month for 12 months by Adrienne Cowling
- winter robin-watch nature walk with Paul and Alysia Krafel
- earth art by Nancy Waldron
- garden border care by Carolyn McHenry
- a two-day houseboat trip by Jack and Patti McIntosh
- window washing by Kathy Hooykaas
- an outdoor portrait session by John Ward Photography

# 1999

A lighted sign with a reader board was constructed at the entrance to the property along Hartnell Avenue. The Board accepted a bid of $203,245 from Peters Construction Company to construct the new wing, which included offices, a bookstore and social hall. The bank loan interest was 9.75%. The church expected construction to be completed by

June. Appliances for the new kitchen were an additional cost of about $11,000.

A grand celebration was held when Rev. Andrea received her doctorate! The church also celebrated Rev. Alice Carpenter's installation as the new Staff Minister.

The church also had a celebration of the new wing on June 26. In addition, the Board approved construction of a sidewalk on the south side of the sanctuary. Thanks to a generous donor, the congregation enjoyed a newly installed water fountain. The Board also approved mini blinds for the new offices. The church gratefully received a $500 tithe from the San Juan Capistrano Church.

The church published the *1999 RCRS Spirit Pages*, a directory with the names and addresses of church members, as well as business ads. The ads announced:
- Shasta Options with Phil Rapin, C.A.S. and Carol Chase-Rapin
- Wise Woman Personal Consultations with Tienne Beaulieu
- World Wide Travel with Dede Burk
- spiritual readings and counsel with Barbara Lilley
- MFTs Patricia Bay and Ann O'Sullivan
- Medley Realty with Bob Huntoon
- certified massage therapists Kathryn Robertson and Julie Marchand
- Milestone Sandblasted River Rocks by Helen Peterson

"Finding Your Way Home" was the name for the family retreat at Camp Latieze.

Rev. Alice led a Mt. Lassen Moonlight Hike.

Arnie Kotler and Therese Fitzgerald, senior students of Thich Nhat Hanh, led a winter mindfulness retreat called, "Cultivating the Mind of Love." The retreat took place at Whiskeytown Environmental School and Camp.

The church purchased an espresso machine to offer espresso-type coffees on Sundays in the social hall.

## 2000

Rev. Carol Chase took the congregation on a "Life is Risky Business" trip cross-country skiing. Not long after, a farewell party for Rev. Carol, who moved to Santa Rosa took place.

New Dimensions Public Radio celebrities, Michael and Justine Toms, presented a seminar.

Mary Manin Morrissey presented her seminar, "Building Your Field of Dreams." It was very well attended and a number of new projects were started by those who attended.

Dr. James taught classes for the Redding Police Department's Chaplain's Academy.

Kelly Carter resigned as Administrative Assistant to complete grad school in Oregon, and the church hired Jeannie Fox as her replacement.

The new Board members elected at the congregational meeting were Leslie Covington, Larry Moore, and Roy Woolfstead.

A spring congregational retreat took place at Camp Latieze revolving around "Love, Serve, and Remember."

A camping site along Antelope Creek on the slopes of Mt. Shasta served as the site for the men's retreat.

A summer white water rafting trip took place on the scenic Klamath River. Only a few people ended up in the river due to the white water plunges, everyone had a joyful experience.

*White Water Rafting Adventure*

Dr. James and Dr. Andrea traveled to Plum Village in France for a retreat with Thich Nhat Hanh.

Dr. Andrea hosted a number of television shows called "Profiles in Faith" for Channel 11, produced by Lynn Fritz. Dr. Andrea also hosted a television show interviewing Mary Manin Morrissey, called "Profiles for Change."

A couples seminar was held entitled "Falling in Love Again."

Dr. James received the Ernest Holmes Award at the annual RSI Conference at Asilomar.

*Enduring Grace* was the focus of the women's retreat, based on a book by the same title about women mystics.

In the fall, don Miguel Ruiz visited the church and presented a seminar on his book *The Four Agreements,* based on Toltec philosophy. A half hour interview hosted by Dr. Andrea with don Miguel aired on Channel 11.

The theme for the Harvest Dinner was "A Funny Thing Happened on the Way to the Forum" and invited all guest to come in Roman costumes.

A New Year's Eve murder mystery party rounded out the year.

## 2001

A *Membership and Services Directory* was published and ads included:
- Tax Preparation and Planning by Deborah Black, EA
- Public Accountant Robert M. Perkins
- Attorneys at Law – Campbell & Clark
- Mac-Co Metal Buildings by Dan Rizzi
- Shasta Software Solutions by Gary German
- Body centered psychotherapy by Barbara Featherstone, MA
- Family counseling services with Phil Rapin, MA, CAS
- Events Extraordinaire with Debbie DeMarias

- State Farm Insurance with Sherry Miller, Agent
- Massage with Kathryn A. Robertson, CMT, Nayla Lewis, Julie Marchand
- Mary Kay cosmetics with Lori A. Heston
- Attitudinal Healing of Redding with Paul Mitchell
- Peer Realty with George S. Peer

The Church held a Buckaroo Services Auction to carpet the hallways in the new wing, purchase a new church sign, and a video projector system for the sanctuary. Auctioned items included:

- auto pin striping by George Willets
- guided fly fishing trip with Tim Harris
- cherry cheesecake by Joann Fay
- dog agility course with Gillian Trumbull
- Italian cream coconut cake by Janell Hunt
- a choir performance at your house by the HeartSangha Choir
- a flower arrangement by Linda Aldrich
- one day of Miata madness touring the north state with Mike Foerster
- swamp cooler service by Dan Rizzi
- snorkel lessons for someone planning to go on the windjammer sailing cruise in the beautiful, blue Caribbean by Chris Hooykaas

Dr. Andrea became the Executive Director of Youth for Religious Science International.

The Gaden Shartse Monks visited and gave three public events that were very well attended. At the same time, the church hosted an Inter-Faith Dialogue with Rev. Heather Hennessey of First Christian Church, Rabbi Yitzhak Nates of Congregation Beth Israel, Geshe Yeshe Phunstok from the Gaden Shartse Monks, and Dr. James Golden. Dharmacharya Lyn Fine presented a public lecture and discussion on bringing mindfulness teachings on love and compassion into daily practice in the tradition of Thich Nhat Hanh, and followed by a Day of Mindfulness.

Gregg Levoy, speaker and author of *Callings: Finding and Following an Authentic Life* presented a seminar.

Dr. James and Dr. Andrea presented a Committed Couples Weekend at the Lost Whale Bed and Breakfast in Trinidad.

Therapist and member, Patty Bay, presented a workshop on healthy relationships using her new book, *Therapy in a Nutshell.*

Julie Marchand organized a Women's Sewing Circle to create a quilt for the front wall of the Sanctuary.

*Handmade Quilt*

A Wilderness Adventure took place at Butte Lake in Lassen Park as a boat-in camping experience using kayaks and canoes to arrive at the campsite.

The church tithed $250 to the Omega Institute to contribute toward the Ram Dass Library Project.

A farewell party was held for Rev. Alice Carpenter when she accepted the position of pastor of the San Jose Church of Religious Science.

In December, Rev. Toni Niemiec was installed as a new Staff Minister.

Rev. Pam Sanchez was named Chaplain Minister.

The Awareness Newsletter was first made available by email.

# 2002

The Heal Line (222-HEAL) started as a community resource where anyone could call 24-hours a day to listen to an affirmative prayer/spiritual mind treatment recording by a minister or practitioner that was updated weekly.

Due to the many new activities taking place in the church, it was decided to terminate the Adopt-A-Highway Program.

The church website address was changed to www.rcrs.org.

Dr. James, Dr. Andrea, Rev. Pam Sanchez, Rev. Alice Carpenter, and Rev. Leslie Gilbertie all attended a special seminar for ministers and chaplains in Mexico with don Miguel Ruiz and his teachers.

Yvonne Day, Leslie Gilbertie, Rev. Pam Sanchez, Mary Schroeder, and Jean Wopat completed the Assistant Chaplain training at Redding Medical Center under the direction of Rev. Art Lillicropp. The new assistants were part of a multi-faith team that then made weekly rounds visiting patients and serving on-call during weekends and holidays at the hospital.

The church joined together with River Oaks Sangha to present a  mindfulness retreat at Camp Latieze with the Nuns of Thich Nhat Hanh's Western Monastery.

A Wilderness Adventure took place on the eastern slopes of Mt. Shasta at Antelope Creek for daring explorers. The experience included solo

*Cooking In The Wilderness*

overnight treks, individual and team orienteering experiences, learning to use GPS for wilderness navigation, group spiritual practices, and plenty of fun.

Five intern practitioners received their licenses at Asilomar in the fall: Joe Neimiec, Sharon Kennedy, Sue Miller, Lynn Fritz, and Barbara Lilley.

A Residential Spiritual Community Committee formed and served as an exploratory venue for members and friends on the idea of living in a spiritual community.

Thanksgiving baskets were prepared and donated to families in the Head Start Program.

Robert Huntoon, one of the founding members of the church died on Christmas morning.

# 2003

In April, Dr. James Golden submitted his resignation as co-pastor followed by divorce proceedings. Dr. Andrea continued as pastor.

Leslie (Gilbertie) Gawain resigned from the Board and Melissa Harris was appointed to the Board to complete Leslie's term. The Board approved a temporary office assistant to work 20 hours a week.

Mary Schroeder received her ministerial license and became a Staff and Chaplain Minister.

Rev. Toni Niemiec received a promotion to Assistant Minister.

Head Start terminated the lease of the cottage in order to move to larger quarters.

The Seva Volunteers were honored with a special dinner celebration.

Alan Cohen presented his "Living Juicy Seminar."

The Gaden Shartse Monks from Dharmasala, India, presented two days of events for the community.

The Buddhist River Oak Sangha offered a walking meditation for peace and non-violence as part of the Season for Non-Violence activities.

Dr. Andrea was elected to the Religious Science International Board of Directors at the annual meeting in Asilomar. Thanks to changes in RSI policy, churches were now allowed to have the number of staff ministers the pastor felt was appropriate. As soon as five ministerial students were licensed, Dr. Andrea announced the addition of five new staff ministers:

- Rev. Yvonne Day
- Rev. Lynn Fritz
- Rev. Sharon Kennedy
- Rev. Sue Miller
- Rev. Joe Neimiec

Rev. Mary Schroeder, Chaplain Minister, published her second book *Engaging Grace: How to use the Power of Co-Creation in Daily Life*.

*Dr. Andrea Golden*

Dr. Andrea completed her training in marriage/family therapy and started a private practice with the Center for Integrative Psychotherapy on Yuba Street.

Rev. Sue Miller and Charlie Born were married on September 20.

# 2004

The year began with a multi-media presentation by Derek Walker Young, the Peace Walker, who spent much of his time walking throughout the world.

Father Leo Booth, a former Episcopal priest, author and lecturer presented an in-depth workshop on recovery and addictive behavior.

Master teacher Roy Eugene Davis presented an evening on meditation based upon the teachings of Paramahansa Yogananda.

Benji Wertheimer, Michael Mandrell and Shiva's Divas offered an exceptional rhythm and chant concert featuring table, acoustic Guitar and outstanding vocals.

Maria Nemeth presented a seminar on her book, *The Energy of Money*.

A special committee of the Board renegotiated the mortgage loan and received a 15-year loan at a fixed rate and no pre-payment penalty.

The Endowment Committee launched their Adopt-a-Piggy Project with 64 plastic piggies that members could fill with pocket change during the year. The funds were placed in the Endowment Fund principle, which would never be spent. An Endowment Regatta, a challenge race with homemade boats cruising across a swimming pool, took place at Roy and Diana Woolfstead's home.

*Floating Boats At The Endowment Fund Regatta*

It was a year of great outdoor activities. Ron Schultz of Shasta County Sierra Club led members and friends on a snowshoe walk for peace around Manzanita Lake in Lassen National Park. A Paddle and Picnic for Peace was held at Castle Lake. A whitewater-rafting trip took place on the Lower Klamath River guided by Turtle River Rafting.

The Hepwa Men's Circle presented a series of gatherings for men in the community. Teachers, Larry Ward and Peggy Rowe Ward led a mindfulness retreat at Whiskeytown Environmental Camp.

Twenty-six members of the choir joined Dr. Andrea at Asilomar during the weeklong conference to sing for her talk in the chapel. The Board recommended that Yvonne Day be licensed as a Chaplain Minister after completing her fourth year ministerial requirements.

The Church sponsored a visit by spiritual leader Ram Dass to be held at the Cascade Theater, but unfortunately Ram Dass had a stroke and the event had to be cancelled.

At year-end, Dr. John Crumbley presented a daylong workshop on "Options to Anger."

## 2005

Rev. Sue led the second annual Snowshoe for Peace Walk at Lassen Park.

Special hats, designed with a top hat logo and a "Hats Off to Life" byline, were sold as fundraisers for Relay for Life, a community cancer project.

After the congregational meeting, the officers elected were:
- Dr. Andrea Golden, President
- Lorre Rizzi, Vice President
- Diana Woolfstead, Secretary
- Charlie Born, Treasurer

The Executive Committee consisted of the officers plus Jim Pernell.

A committee led by Jim Nelson and Mary Schroeder held several community meetings to develop a five-year strategic plan.

A six-month experiment changed the Awareness Newsletter publication to every other month with very brief articles, but by the end of the year it was back to monthly production in full size.

The Church held a regional meeting of practitioners, called "Become a Healer—The Practitioner's Journey." Forty-one practitioners from all over northern California attended and enjoyed workshops created by the Redding ministers and practitioners, along with a delicious lunch.

A program for the Season of Nonviolence included profiles and discussion groups on Albert Einstein, Thich Nhat Hanh, Fierce Grace, and Aung San Suu Kyi.

The Center launched an Adopt-a-Soldier Program and prepared care packages for soldiers being sent to Baghdad.

In September, the Gaden Shartze Tibetan Monks performed a cultural event as well as offering personal healing sessions. Tulku Lobsang Jinpa Rinpoche offered a workshop on "Death, Bardo, and Rebirth—the Three Stages of Life."

Rev. Sue MillerBorn officiating at Dr. Andrea Golden and Joe Asebedo's wedding at the Spiritual Enrichment Center.

In October, Dr. Andrea and Joe Asebedo were married in a beautiful ceremony at the church. While on their honeymoon, guest speakers were Rev. Jaine Ryder of Bellingham, Washington and Dr. Jeffrey Proctor of Baltimore, Maryland. Both offered Sunday talks and afternoon workshops.

Doug Von Koss presented an evening of poetry and music.

Benji and Heather Wertheimer and Manose graced our stage with international music.

## 2006

The Center's Abundance Drive fundraiser focused on maximizing the beauty of the grounds and facilities by creating a boutique-wedding venue. New Board members were Deb Black, Ace Clemens, and Sherry Miller.

The Center celebrated Rev. Pam Sanchez's ordination.

In September, Rev. Mary Schroeder and Paul Mitchell were married with Rev. Sue MillerBorn officiating.

Outside speakers invited to present seminars and workshops during the year included:
- Medical scientist, psychologist, author of eleven books, Joan Borysenko, Ph.D., presented a workshop.
- Motivational speaker and transformational workshop leader, David A. Jones, offered a three-day workshop on "Free the Heart."
- The Nuns of Deer Park Monastery helped facilitate the Mindfulness Retreat at Camp Latieze, called "Calming the Fearful Mind."
- Mary Manin Morrissey gave a powerful seminar on "Living the Life You Love."
- Pianist, composer, and producer, Peter Kater, performed his stunning music.

The cottage was upgraded to meet ADA requirements.

The Board approved the name change from Redding Church of Religious Science to dba Spiritual Enrichment Center.

## SPIRITUAL ENRICHMENT CENTER

2006 was the first year for the event Floating of the Lanterns, organized by Rev. Lynn Fritz. The lanterns were designed and crafted by Doug Hoerber, architect extraordinaire. Each lantern had one of several interfaith prayers on it. The lanterns were lit with candles and floated in the pond along Park Marina Drive in the evening thanks to a few members who kept them corralled with their kayaks.

RCRS membership in 2006 was 371.

Dozens of members and friends kept active with geo cashing travel bug adventures, a Rogue River raft trip, and a Prairie Creek camping trip.

Center ministers presented a six-week Wednesday evening healing service.

The Center showed a very popular movie, "Down the Rabbit Hole: What the Bleep?" that was followed with an extensive discussion.

The women's retreat took place at the Windmill Inn in Ashland, Oregon.

Rev. Dr. Candice Beckett spoke at Sunday services while Dr. Andrea and Joe Asebedo enjoyed their first wedding anniversary.

Tienne Beaulieu received her practitioner license.

## 2007

The Center welcomed Rev. Sue MillerBorn as Co-Pastor with Dr. Andrea.

February 18, 2007 Mile 1320 After a gruelling climb the SEC walkers reach the Continental Divide in Colorado. It was cold, so after a short rest they moved on.

Sandy Babcock, RN, started the "Walk Around The World" program to get everyone out walking for the summer. At each hike, the mileage walked was calculated and a photo taken of the participants. Gene Knabel added a background to the photo based on the location the group was theoretically at in their walk around the world. At one point everyone was bobbing about in the middle of the ocean! Everyone enjoyed the travel photos that were posted in the social hall. Sandy also developed a Health Ministry with a health survey for the congregation to identify other focused activities that would be beneficial.

A farewell party for Rev. Joe and Rev. Toni Niemiec celebrated their time at the Center with a great sendoff to Spokane, Washington where they accepted the positions of co-pastors of that church.

The Center updated the strategic plan with the assistance of Rev. Mary Mitchell and Jim Nelson.

A fundraising program was focused on beautifying and upgrading the property behind the sanctuary.

Dr. Amit Goswami, Ph.D., professor emeritus from the University of Oregon presented a seminar on "Quantum Physics and the Teachings of Jesus."

The Center completed the first phase makeover of the Center gardens, and the second phase was to re-orient the playground and begin work on a trellis project.

The Endowment Fund awarded grants of $4,000 to worthy Center-related projects.

The movie "The Secret" was such a worldwide hit that Dr. Andrea and Rev. Lynn Fritz held an evening viewing and discussion session.

During the summer, Nancy Pernell and Jill Boland offered "Voices of the Bioneers," a six-week inspirational course.

The men's conference, "A Man's Journey to the Sacred Pool" took place at Trinity Mountains Resort.

Several outstanding guest speakers came to the Center during the year, including:

- Jean Houston, who presented her seminar on "The Mystery of Purpose and Destiny."
- Jonathan Young, Ph.D. and curator of the Joseph Campbell Archives offered a seminar on "Discovering Our Personal Mythology."
- Gary Gardner, Director of Research Worldwatch Institute held a program on "Inspiring Progress: Religions' Contribution to Sustainable Development."
- John Mahoney presented a one-man performance on Henry David Thoreau.

Linda Covich led a project called "Empty Bowls," where participants created and decorated a pottery bowl at a local shop and then auctioned their bowls as a fundraiser at a soup dinner. An amazing array of decorations and colors created quite an assortment of bowls.

Dr. Andrea and Rev. Sue ended the year with a retreat offering, "Entering the Sanctuary of the Heart."

## 2008

The year began with Snowshoes for Peace led by Rev. Sue MillerBorn.

Bill Parr began a fundraiser to construct a labyrinth by cycling cross-country, from the west coast to the east coast!

In March, Dr. Andrea announced her planned retirement with this letter to the congregation:

March 1, 2008

Dear Spiritual Friend,

I am writing to tell you of a very important decision I have made. I have decided that it is now time for me to relinquish my role as the senior minister of our beautiful spiritual community. My last day as senior minister will be August 15, 2008. The good news is that I am not leaving our community, only stepping in to a less active role!

I am sure some of you are asking why, and I wanted to have the opportunity to tell you myself. I am at a time in my life where "time" seems very precious. As you probably know, ministry is extremely consuming, and while I have been deeply gratified to serve you in this way, I recently became a grandmother. I have a lovely husband and son that I do not see as much as I would like, and my older children are spread out in a way that makes it difficult to visit them without more "time." I am also ready to write, meditate, and deepen my connection to Spirit—and that takes "time!"

Believe me, this decision is perhaps the most difficult one I have ever made in my life. I love you; I love our spiritual community, and I love what the Spiritual Enrichment Center stands for here in Redding and the larger world. That is why I am staying on to serve our community, although in a different role. My husband,

Joe and son Daniel, will also remain a vital part of our Center, and you will see the three of us doing SEVA often.

I hope you will join me in welcoming with open arms our new minister in August. Whoever that may be, they are going to be the luckiest minister in the world because they will be serving an incredible, spiritually mature, and loving congregation.

We have six months to celebrate, anticipate, and take the next evolutionary leap together! I hope I will have the opportunity to share this time with you. Thank you for letting me serve as your senior minister.

Many Blessings,

Dr. Andrea Asebedo

A Minister Search Committee was formed with Charlie Born as Chair and Rev. Mary Mitchell, Vice Chair. A congregational survey was developed to get a better understanding of what the community was looking for in a new minister. One hundred and ten people completed the congregational survey. Dr. Andrea wrote and distributed a beautiful treatment for everyone to attract the perfect pastor.

The Endowment Committee voted to spend some of the investment earnings for the Youth group, a drinking fountain in the social hall, a stage monitor, wireless microphone, outdoor lighting, and the labyrinth project.

Joe Asebedo and Brian Cummings began a men's group.

A celebration with great fanfare took place for Mary Mitchell's ordination.

A memorial walk honored the passing of Phil Aldrich.

Later in the year the congregation also honored the passing of Larry Miller and Dede Dixon.

A minister from the east coast was an early candidate for the pastor position, but dropped out before the vote was held. Rev. Judith Churchman and Rev. Bob Luckin were the other candidates for the position. The vote took place in June, with Rev. Judith and Rev. Bob elected as the Center's new co-pastors.

On August 16, 2008, the congregation celebrated the retirement of Rev. Dr. Andrea Asebedo, a noted Emerson Scholar, student of Thich Naht Hanh, story teller, builder of community, gifted communicator and teacher. The invitation headlined the quote of St. Francis of Assisi, "It is no use walking anywhere to preach unless our walking is our preaching." Entitled "The Journey," the celebration included a potluck buffet, live music, dancing, and honoring of Rev. Dr. Andrea.

## JUDITH CHURCHMAN AND BOB LUCKIN

*Rev. Judith Churchman
And Rev. Bob Luckin*

In September, new co-pastors Rev. Judith Churchman and her husband Rev. Bob Luckin arrived in Redding. A get-acquainted evening of wine and food was held to celebrate their installation. The co-pastor team came from the Monterey, California Church of Religious Science. Prior to that Rev. Judith was pastor of the Paradise Church of Religious Science, and Rev. Bob founded the Oroville Church of Religious Science.

A special presenter this year was Joan Borysenko, a world-wide expert in the mind/body connection, who presented the workshop "Saying Yes to Change: Essential Wisdom for Your Journey." Karen Drucker provided the inspirational music at the workshop. The Redding Searchlight highlighted the workshop in the Health Section of the newspaper with a two-third page article entitled "A healing touch: Patients find power in prayer, meditation, and healing therapy." Above the article was a photo of members Sandy Babcock, RN conducting healing touch on Reva Malson, to help her cope with the side effects of chemotherapy. An adjacent article on Joan's visit was entitled "Author urges people to Say Yes to Change."

The Redding Record Searchlight began a section called "Voices of Faith," which invited ministers or leaders of various faith traditions to submit their answers to weekly questions developed by newspaper staff. Rev. Lynn Fritz and Rev. Judith Churchman alternated weeks writing for the column.

When Rev. Heather Hennessey retired at First Christian Church and as Chair of the Shasta County Interfaith Forum, Rev. Lynn was elected as chair. The Forum invited ministers or leaders of various faith traditions to meet monthly and share activities and information.

# 2009

A guided meditation was added to the 9:00 a.m. Sunday service.

Use of the cottage for healing arts professionals during the week met Board approval.

After several years of negotiations and discussion, the two parent organizations teaching Science of Mind officially merged: International Centers for Spiritual Living and United Centers for Spiritual Living, to simply be called Centers for Spiritual Living (CSL) based in Golden, Colorado. The Board signed an affiliation agreement with CSL, and the name of the church was changed to Center for Spiritual Living, Redding.

The Endowment Committee voted to spend some of the investment earnings for a video projector, a software upgrade, and new lights for the sanctuary. John Maxwell Taylor visited and presented a workshop on his book "The Power of I AM."

Membership at this time was 410.

Lorre Rizzi resigned from the Board and Linda Aldrich stepped in to take the rest of her term.

The labyrinth now had a fountain, thanks to a donation.

Long-time practitioner Tienne Beaulieu resigned from her duties at the Center to take the position of Choir Director for All Saints Episcopal Church.

A men's retreat featured guest speaker Doug Von Koss.

Rev. Bob held a pet blessing that had good attendance. He also did a handwriting analysis workshop.

Cher Matthews led a committee to set up a booth at the Redding Chamber of Commerce Annual Business Expo at the Convention Center.

Dr. Andrea Asebedo's ministerial position with the Center was changed from Staff Minister to the honorable Minister Emeritus.

For the Conscious Giving Program/Pledge Program rally for the year, Rev. Bob recorded a healing CD and made it available to everyone in the congregation. It was called "There is No Place like Home" and featured the following prosperity treatment:

> Abundance is the nature of God. Throughout all creation, abundance is the rule. The number of galaxies that exist is beyond our comprehension. The number of stars in each galaxy is beyond counting. Everywhere we look in nature there is an abundance of plant and animal species, each finding a unique way of expressing life. Knowing that abundance is God's nature and that I am an individualized expression God, it follows that to experience abundance is my nature. I accept that for myself now, in the form of an abundance of love, peace, and money. I know that if I am experiencing a lack in my life it is because I have blocked the natural good that is mine. I choose to allow the flow of money into my life so I may express life more fully.

I know I am the Beloved of God, and it is the Father's good pleasure to give me all I can accept. I accept my good. I claim it now. Thank you, God. And so it is.

## 2010

Rev. Judith and Rev. Bob appointed Rev. Mary Mitchell and Rev. Sue MillerBorn as Assistant Ministers.

For a period, the Awareness Newsletter was only distributed through the Internet, but the continued request for hard copies resulted in a resumption of mailing, although to a smaller mailing list.

The Endowment Committee voted to fund projects out of investment earnings for young adult services, sending youth leaders to camp, and energy-saving fluorescent lights.

A discussion regarding the design of the labyrinth resulted in the development of a template for a pattern.

"A Ticket and a Tile" was a fundraising campaign to raise money to replace the roof over the sanctuary. After researching various types of roofing materials, the Board selected a composition roof and paid for it with the funds raised, which was close to $20,000. The roof proved to be the most practical and economical.

An organic garden committee formed and members brought vegetables on Sunday during the summer to sell on a love offering basis. The revenue benefitted both the Good News Rescue Mission and People of Progress.

Dr. Lisa Love presented her workshop "Beyond the Secret: the Spiritual Power and the Law of Attraction."

The Board developed an in-depth survey that included all aspects of the Center, which was followed by an update of the five-year strategic plan.

The Center realized significant savings when Rev. Bob renegotiated the copier lease.

The Redding Record Searchlight published a long article with a photo and architectural drawing of the new labyrinth to be dedicated on September 24. Darcia Slape wrote the excellent article for the newspaper. A plaque placed next to the labyrinth honoring Dr. Andrea Asebedo.

Rod Loomis and Rev. Sandy Freeman-Loomis presented "The God Dialogue," a mini-play performed during the Sunday service that was delightful and very well received.

The Center decided that the hand-made quilt would hang in the front of the sanctuary from November until spring, to then be replaced with the cloud paintings created by artist and friend, Rebecca Lowell.

# 2011

Mellon Thomas Benedict presented a workshop "Beyond: Lighten Up!" about his near death experience and vision of the earth in the future.

A fundraiser took place to benefit the people of Japan after the earthquake and tsunami devastation.

At the recommendation of the insurance company, all of the solid doors in the office and the side room in the sanctuary had new windows added.

Elders and parents with children had twelve parking places designated for them on the side of the sanctuary. Thanks to the Maintenance Team, the whole parking lot was restriped. In other areas of maintenance, the Children's Cottage realized a new floor. The leak in the side practitioner room required removal and replacement of part of the wall. The front right of the sanctuary had a new plasma TV screen to show announcements and words to the congregational songs.

The congregation celebrated two ordinations this year, one for Rev. Sue MillerBorn and another for Rev. Lynn Fritz. Both were outstanding events.

Practitioner and Youth Group Leader, Ace Clemens, traveled to Malawi, Africa, with youth from RSI to help build school buildings. This is a special project by teens in the world-wide organization and has been a tremendous asset to the children of Malawi.

The Endowment Committee voting members for 2011 were:
· Gillian Trumbull, chair
· Deb Black
· Charlie Born
· Kurt Mitchell
· Jim Pernell

Those that stepped down as voting members were Tara Steele, Roy Woolfstead, and Lorre Rizzi. The Endowment Committee grants for improvements in the Center went to a new computer for the sound booth, sending Youth Leaders to camp, and replacing the cottage deck.

Wednesday evening services were started on a six-month trial with a rotation of ministers presenting their own programs.

The Center purchased SEVA T-shirts in a bright blue color for those to wear when helping with community outreach projects.

At the congregational meeting, members who made their transition during the previous year were honored. They were: Reva Malson, George Willits, Frannie Aldrich, and Lloyd Fox.

New intern practitioners were announced: Diana Bordeaux, Charlie Born, Marylin Miller, and Tara Steele.

# 2012

A Congregational Survey Committee completed the survey of members and friends regarding their desires for the community. The Board received the result a few months later for their review.

Loren Swift, a certified trainer in non-violent communication, presented a very well-attended workshop on "Embodying the Heart of NVC Consciousness: Deepening the Practice of Living in Unity."

A SEVA Appreciation Dinner took place in March with all of the food prepared by the Board of Trustees as a thank you to all who contribute their time and energy to make the Center a success.

Jim and Nancy Pernell financed the replacement of all lights in the facilities with energy-saving lights.

The Endowment Fund made $4,000 available for grant awards that were primarily used to upgrade the computer system in the office.

New Board members elected at the congregational meeting were Cher Matthews and Kurt Mitchell.

Lorie Barnes, Administrative Assistant, moved to Bellingham, Washington and the Board hired Tara Steele as her replacement.

Long time Youth Coordinators Ace Clemens and Erin Szymanski also moved to Bellingham.

At the congregational meeting, Rev. Judith presented the following report:

### Review of 2011 and Plans for 2012

Our Mission: Empowering abundant, spirit-connected lives through sacred service, community, and Science of Mind Principles.

Your Center leadership has developed the following plan to expand our vision for a greater awareness and practice of Science of Mind in Northern California and throughout the world. We are grateful for the past year and look forward to an even greater year of service to this community and beyond in 2012. We invite you to join in this journey of awakening and celebration.

## The Commitment of our Community
*"The moment one definitely commits oneself, then Providence moves too."*

William Hutchison Murray, "The Scottish Himalayan Expedition" (1951)

Members and friends of the Center for Spiritual Living, Redding committed $145,000 in financial support to our community in 2012. We project an additional $121,479 income from classes, events, and other sources to meet our 2012 operational budget of $266,479.

## Our Sunday Plan for Sacred Services
*"Sangha is not a building, it is a consciousness held by a collective group that welcomes, celebrates, and honors you just the way you are. You'll know it because it is as if you have walked into a wall of love, immersing you in it in the most amazing way."*
Dennis Merritt Jones, "The Art of Being"

We are committed to offering two life-changing Sacred Services every Sunday morning. Last year we provided 141 services including 35 Wednesday Night Sacred Services, a Thanksgiving Eve Taize service, and our beautiful Christmas Eve candle-lighting service. We have 328 members, and over the past year a large number of visitors joined in services at our Center for the first time. Sundays also include connection and inspiration for our youth. We offer a full program for nursery through pre-teens in the morning with the teens meeting in the afternoons. Our prayer treatment ministry after the Sunday services is a gift from all practitioners to anyone who wants to heal a hurt or build a dream. Our entire community is invited to walk our impressive labyrinth at any time, and we have had several planned labyrinth walks for our community. Silent meditation is available in our beautiful Meditation Pavilion. All who share in these extraordinary gatherings have experienced outstanding music, heart-felt personal testimonials from members sharing how prayer has changed their lives, and lessons in Spiritual Principle for both children and adults to support our living fuller, richer, and more meaningful lives.

## Spiritual Enrichment and Education
*"Where the mind is without fear and the head is held high."*
Rabindrath Tagore

We commit to provide a myriad of opportunities to deepen our understanding and application of spiritual principle in 2012.

### Classes
Our Center is abundant in life-enriching classes. Rev. Bob Luckin is teaching the SOM 100 series on Tuesday nights. Rev. Judith Churchman and our Assistant and Staff ministers teach the SOM 200 series. Rev. Judith is teaching Troward's Edinburg Lectures currently, and Rev. Sue MillerBorn began her class on Emma Curtis Hopkins in March. Rev. Mary Mitchell is teaching SOM 300, and Rev. Judith completed a SOM 350 practicum this year. Revs. Bob and Judith facilitate Creative Living Classes. Rev. Judith provides an Essential Self Saturday once a month class, and Rev. Bob is facilitating A Course in Miracles discussion group, as well as two support groups, one for those experiencing depression and one for those living with cancer. A whole new array of classes will be offered in the fall.

### Retreats
Retreats are a hallmark of our Center with our beautiful facilities and at other retreat centers in Northern California. Last year we held a Mediation Retreat, a Family Retreat, A Course in Miracles Retreat, a Women's Retreat, and an Everyday Miracles Retreat. In 2012, we have planned a Meditation Retreat, a

Couples Retreat, a Silent Retreat, a Women's Retreat, a Family Retreat, and a Practical Mystics Retreat.

**HeartSangha Choir**
Music is a very important aspect of celebration. For anyone who loves to sing, the choir meets on Thursday nights. It is a great place to gain confidence in singing in public, to meet new people, make life-long friendships, have fun, and be part of presenting inspirational music twice a month.

**Workshops, Concerts and other Activities**
The Center hosts a number of workshops, seminars, and concerts. The schedule this year includes Dr. Lisa Love in January, Dave DeLuca in February, Gary Simmons in March, Terry McBride in May, and hopefully Neale Donald Walsh in the fall. We have enjoyed Anton Mizerak and Laura Berryhill, as well as Dwaine Briggs.

**Our Commitment to Youth**
*"Children are the hands by which we take hold of heaven."*

Henry Ward Beecher

This year the Children's Church is under new group leadership. We thank Wendi Stewart profusely for her dedicated service in that role during the past year. Her work schedule demanded that she step down and be a part of the program as a teacher. Our Council Leadership now includes Rev. Kay Stewart, Rev. Sue MillerBorn, and Kelly Rizzi. This dynamic group is breathing new excitement into our Children's Church. They are creating new curricula and coordinating the topics to match the Sunday lessons so that parents can discuss the ideas with their children at home. They are communicating with the parents about what lessons are taught and when. There will be separate lessons for the different age groups: Babies 0–3; Lights, ages 4–7; Tweens, 8– 12; and teens, ages 13–18, who meet Sunday afternoons. Our teens have been under the excellent leadership of Ace

Clemens. Ace plans to move this year, probably in the summer. We are calling for a new Youth Director for our teen group.

## Community Feasting

*"Peace be unto thee stranger, enter and be not afraid.... The table is laid, and the fruits of Life are spread before thee."*

Ernest Holmes, *The Science of Mind* (1938)

We love to socialize and each Sunday after services, we offer the opportunity to enjoy beverages and snacks in a time of fellowship. Class nights almost always include snacks. We honored our Sevites (Seva Volunteers) in March with a delicious, Italian dinner cooked and provided by your Board of Trustees. Our annual Harvest Dinner is a feast, and this spring we plan to indulge in a Spring Bounty Dinner & Dance on May 18th. Our Quarterly "Friday Night at the Movies" always begins with a meal. Annually we have gone to Patrick's Point for a weekend summer camp out, which includes all the meals. We enjoy several dinner/dances each year, including New Year's Eve.

## Our Gift in the World

*"In truth, spiritual community is necessary for us to be able to fulfill our purpose here on Earth. We need one another to enhance God's experience of loving Itself."* Dr. Dennis Merritt Jones, "The Art of Being"

As we share Science of Mind with the world, we are committed to supporting our spiritual movement in a world-class manner. Resources allow participation in Centers for Spiritual Living conferences. We support our parent organization, Centers for Spiritual Living, with voluntary giving. Headquarters provides curriculum, licensing, conferences, and a global community that together brings Science of Mind to the world.

We participate in our local community in many ways. In February, we distributed 150 backpacks filled with sweaters and coats to the homeless. We are participating in Project Hope, providing coats, sweaters, and bedding to the homeless. We support the Salvation Army by giving gifts for needy children with the Angel Tree. Last year we participated in the Relay for Life Cancer Walk to raise money for cancer research, and the Alzheimer's Walk for Alzheimer's research.

In late March, co-pastors Rev. Judith Churchman and Rev. Bob Luckin gave notice of their retirement effective May 31st to be followed by a move to Florida to be closer to family. They generously donated all of their books and bookcases to the Center, which became a lending library in the side room off the sanctuary. A plaque honoring Rev. Judith and Rev. Bob was added to the lending library.

The congregation celebrated newly licensed practitioners Marylin Miller and Tara Steele, as well as new intern practitioners Bonnie Metcalf, Amy Silberstein, Darcia Slape, and Katie Watters.

## REV. SUE MILLERBORN AND REV. MARY MITCHELL
The two Assistant Ministers and three Staff Ministers prepared a proposal to the Board of Trustees to run the Center during the interim period until a new Senior Minister was hired. The board concurred and Assistant Ministers Rev. Mary Mitchell and Rev. Sue MillerBorn were hired as part-time Interim Co-Pastors to handle all of the administration and operations of the Center. Mary and Sue, as well as the three staff ministers, Rev. Sharon Kennedy, Rev. Kay Stewart, and Rev. Pam Sanchez would share the presentations of Sunday lessons.

*Rev. Sue MillerBorn*                    *Rev. Mary Mitchell*

Upon the recommendation of CSL Headquarters, to begin healing the past and re-centering the congregation on the future, the Co-Pastors were asked to hold co-creation meetings, based on a specific process. A trained facilitator, Rev. Eileen Brownell of the Greater Chico Center for Spiritual Living, was hired for this work. After two meetings, it was apparent that the process was not a good fit for this congregation, and Mary and Sue developed a different process in collaboration with Phoebe Fazio, called the "Completion vs. Finished Process," which proved to be a success.

Mary and Sue began weekly emails to congregants to update everyone about what happened at the Center during the week. Personnel Policies were created and approved by the board, including a separate sexual harassment policy. Thanks to Board member Gene Rand, an Emergency Action Plan was created.

By the end of the year, Tara Steele decided to leave her position as Administrative Assistant to take ministerial training at the Holmes

Institute in Santa Rosa, and coincidently Lorie Barnes returned to Redding the following week and resumed the Administrative Assistant position.

In December, the Board of Trustees appointed a Minister Search Committee members included:

- Co-chair Charlie Born
- Co-chair Rev. Mary Mitchell
- Harry Bleile
- Hazel Hughes
- Marylin Miller
- Carolyn Pearson
- Traci Roberti
- Gillian Trumbull
- Fred Erickson
- Roy Woolfstead

The Committee prepared a Center Profile, which was posted on the CSL Headquarters Open Pulpit web page, a questionnaire to be completed by candidates, and a draft Letter of Call.

In the Center Profile, the Center was described as follows:

**1. Name and Location:**    Center for Spiritual Living, Redding
1905 Hartnell Avenue
Redding, CA 96002
(530) 221-4849 Fax (530) 221-4840
Website: www.cslredding.org

**2. Purpose or Goals:**

Vision:                 Celebrating our Spiritual Magnificence

Mission:                Empowering individuals to live an abundant, spirit-connected life through sacred service, community, and Science of Mind® principles

Words of Purpose:       Enrichment and Growth

## 3. Specific qualifications we desire in our Minister:

Leadership: Authentic, confident, passionate, integrity, competent, shared leadership with respect and honesty, experience leading a large congregation, non-judgmental, empowers others, good communicator, ability to be a pastor and executive director, demonstrates Science of Mind principles and inspires others to do the same, unwavering by the appearance of duality, genuinely embrace the community, connected and centered in love.

Speaking: Articulate, knowledgeable, a dynamic and enjoyable speaker who opens us to ourselves and guides us deeper, a clear message, able to laugh at oneself, inspirational, inspires others to connect with their highest essence, invokes in others "aha" moments, and a heart centered presentation style.

Teaching: Aligned with Universal Truth and able to awaken this attribute in others, helps students connect with their Divine Knowing, open at the top to receive whatever is needed to be expressed, organized, well read, able to apply teachings to daily living, able to share from the heart and from experience, refers often to Science of Mind principles in new ways that provoke thought and discussion, brings in other traditions and Eastern and Western philosophies with Science of Mind as the starting point—but not the only point.

Spiritual Attributes: Exemplifies the principles of Science of Mind, stays centered in Oneness and sees truth in all human situations, integrity, passionate, sincere, deeply committed to deep regular spiritual practice, compassionate, Science of Mind principles combined with the wisdom of other religions and Eastern and Western philosophies, kind, sincere, grounded.

## 4. Church Statistics
   A.  Year Founded: Church charter in 1978


   B.  Number of Licensed Practitioners:
       2 – Interim Co-Pastors (previously Assistant Ministers)
       3 – Staff Ministers

       2 – Licensed Practitioners
       5 – Intern Practitioners

C. Paid Staff:
       2 – Interim Co-Pastors part time
       1 -- Financial, Facilities, and Bookstore Manager 40 hours/week
       1 – Administrative Assistant 32 hours/week
       1 - Music Director, part time
       1 – Choir Director, part time
       1 – Child Care for Nursery, part time
       1 – Bookstore Assistant, part time
       1 – Webmaster, part time

D. Board of Trustees:
Currently one of the interim co-pastors is the President of the nine-member Board. Board members serve three-year terms. The current Board is made up of six women and three men, all long-time members with professional expertise and includes a teacher, office worker, business owner, nurse, banker, engineer, and real estate agent.

E. Registered Membership: 325

F. Average Sunday attendance: 45 – 50 at 9:00 service and 110 – 145 at 10:30 service.

G. Average children/youth attendance: 1-15 children, five youth

H. Average New Midweek Service attendance: There is no midweek service at this time.

I. Accredited Science of Mind classes being offered at this time:

January 2013: 1 New Foundations (evening), 2 Building a Healing Consciousness (one evening, one day), 1 Visioning (evening)

## 5. Ministry:

A survey taken in spring 2012 showed the Center serves a congregation of 77% women. Survey respondents have been coming to the Center for over 10 years and 70% are members. 87% of the respondents do daily spiritual practices and 12% do so 2 – 3 times each week.

Income range: $10 – 30,000 = 29%; $30 – 50,000 = 25%; $51 – 100,000 =2 9%; over $100,000 = 17%.

Age range: 18 – 87

Interests: Science of Mind classes, non-accredited classes and workshops, socials, retreats, annual dinners, used book sales, attending community theater, camping, Seva (selfless service to God).

Community Outreach: American Cancer Society Daffodil Days, Relay for Life (for cancer research), Walk to End Alzheimer's, Ducky Derby, City Creek Clean-Up, Salvation Army Giving Tree, Shoes for Souls, Food for Hope, Shasta County Interfaith Forum, and others.

Ministries: Chaplain, Health Ministry, Congregational Support, Community Outreach, Children and Youth Programs.

Leadership Team: Although the leadership structure is primarily the co-pastors and the Board, leadership is more of a circle than a pyramid. This team is made up of approximately 25 – 30 people who lead or participate in volunteer teams called Seva Teams.

Seva Teams: Seva, a Sanskrit word meaning selfless service to God, is very important in the Center. About 150 people serve on 17 Seva Teams, which includes Awareness (newsletter) Mailing, Awareness Bookstore, Children's Church, HeartSangha Choir, Cleaning, Congregational Support, Endowment, Friendship/Membership, Health, Landscape, Building Maintenance, Pledge, Prosperity, Publicity, Special Events, Seva Coordination, Audio/Video, Ushers and Greeters, Office/Administrative.

## 6. Facility:

The Center's property is 3.9 acres that includes a 1.6-acre floodplain dedicated to the City of Redding. The 2.3-acre balance of property is L-shaped. The parking lot has 97 striped spaces. The Center facilities include three buildings:

> Main Building: sanctuary, lobby, and restrooms – 5,304 sq. ft., plus:
> Bookstore – 361 sq. ft.
> Offices – (3) 436 sq. ft.
> Admin area and work room – 330 sq. ft.
> Social Hall – 840 sq. ft.
> Kitchen – 264 sq. ft.
> Children/Healing Art Cottage has 3 rooms: kitchenette, restroom – 904 sq. ft.
> Meditation Pavilion – 581 sq. ft.

Value: Land $280,000. Buildings $970,000. Equipment $107,685. The original mortgage was $500,000. As of 12/31/12, the Center's mortgage is $281,857 of which $95,400 is owed to families at a 3% interest rate, the balance to Tri Counties Bank at a 5% interest rate to be paid off in 7 years.

> Classes are held in all of the buildings. Seating:
> Sanctuary – 400 standing capacity, 200 with chairs
> Social Hall – 70 in chairs, 50 at tables
> Cottage – 20 in chairs, 10 at tables
> Pavilion – 25 – 30 in chairs and benches or cushions

## 7. Locale:

Redding is a city in far-northern California, located on Interstate 5 about 150 miles north of Sacramento, which is the capital of California. Redding is nestled at the very northwestern end of the Great Central Valley, which transitions into the Cascade foothills. Mountains are to the north, east, and west, with fertile farmland to the south, surround the city.

Redding's unique location is due to the Sacramento River, which courses through the city. It is the county seat of Shasta County, California. With a population of 89,861 as of the 2010 Census, Redding is the largest city in the Shasta Cascade region and is the fourth largest city in the Sacramento Valley.

Redding and Shasta County are major centers for outdoor recreation activities. Northern California offers wide-open spaces, true wilderness, snow-capped mountains, pristine lakes, prairie swaths of forest and eerie volcanic landscapes. Photographic opportunities throughout the region abound.

The City of Redding boasts 529 acres of parkland including the magnificent Sacramento River Trail system. That, joined with the 400 acres of parks just south in the City of Anderson, affords over 80 miles of trails for hiking, biking, birding, and in Anderson River Park and the Clear Creek Greenway—horseback riding. Fishing is a popular pastime in the major creeks and Sacramento River. Both cities have golf and disc golf courses. The third largest city in the county, Shasta Lake, is just north of Redding is home to Shasta Lake, a 30,000-acre lake with 370 miles of shoreline. The lake is a houseboat mecca with 10 marinas.

Minutes west of Redding, Whiskeytown National Recreation Area offers 70 miles of trails that include four scenic waterfalls. Kayaking and sailing are popular on the 3,200-acre lake with 370 miles of shoreline. An hour east of Redding is Mt. Lassen Volcanic National Park with 150 miles of trails. The dominant feature of the park is Lassen Peak, the largest plug dome volcano in the world and the southern-most volcano in the Cascade Range. Some trails lead through bubbling mud pots and sulfurous fumes of this active volcano.

There are seven national forests within the greater region where camping, hiking, fishing, hunting, river rafting, and true wilderness experiences are enjoyed. The north state region that includes Redding offers nearly every outdoor recreation opportunity that anyone can imagine.

Redding has a Mediterranean climate, with hot summers and cold and wet winters. Winter (November – April) provides the most precipitation of any season when the weather tends to be either rainy or foggy with occasional light snow. Summers are hot and dry, but rain is possible, usually with a thunderstorm. The average daily maximum temperature in July stays near 100 – 105 degrees Fahrenheit (38 degrees Celsius). The highest official recorded temperature in Redding was 118 degrees Fahrenheit (48 degrees Celsius) on July 20, 1988. Redding has an average possible sunshine of 88%, the second-highest percentage (after Yuma, Arizona) of any US city.

The greater Redding community consists of 48% males and 52% females with a median resident age of 38.5 years. Redding median household income for 2009 was $45,830 compared to the California median of $58,931. The estimated median house or condo value in 2009 was $244,500. Ethnicity of Redding is 81.3% white, 8.7% Hispanic, 1.9% American Indian, 1.1% Black, and 3.3% Asian. Unemployment for the past few years has averaged 13 – 15%.

Redding is home to two large hospitals, Mercy (a Dignity Health hospital) and Shasta Regional Medical Center, and the smaller acute care Patients' Hospital. The Redding Municipal Airport has two carriers, United Express and Horizon Air. In education, Redding is home to four-year degree Simpson University, and Shasta Community College, as well as Shasta Bible College and Graduate School, and National University.

Sources for more information:
> www.sclredding.org
> www.city-date.com/city/Redding-California.html
> www.ci.redding.ca.us/demographics.html
> http://www.shastacascade.com/

**8. Salary range offered:** A base of $50,000 per year of which $25,000 is the housing allowance, plus a split on classes and workshops. An incentive program is negotiable.

**9. Benefits available:** A health savings account, retirement contribution, two conferences each year. Moving expenses are dependent on funds available.

**10. Reason for pulpit vacancy and how long vacant:**
Rev. Judith Churchman and Rev. Bob Luckin retired after serving as co-pastors from 2008 to May 30, 1012. Assistant Minister, Rev. Sue MillerBorn and Rev. Mary Mitchell, stepped in as Interim Co-Pastors on June 1, 2012 until the Center hires a new Senior Minister.

**11. Number of Senior Ministers in the last ten years:**
1981—2003 Rev. Dr. James Golden
1988—2008 Rev. Dr. Andrea Golden
2008—2012 Rev. Judith Churchman and Rev. Bob Luckin
2012—Interim Ministers: Rev. Sue MillerBorn and Rev. Mary Mitchell

**12. What is the general financial condition of the church?**
The Center is financially healthy with a positive annual income. The 2012 General Fund budget was $238,673. The 2013 General Fund budget is $238,060.

**13. Does the church have any current or past due debts? If so, please list total amount and the monthly debt service amount**
The only debts are the mortgage, loans to pay down the mortgage, and contract commitment for the copier and postage machine. These total $3,600 per month plus the plan to save $1,000 per month to eventually pay back the personal loans.
Is anything owed the previous minister? No.

**14. Are you offering travel expenses and or speaking and workshop presentation fees to your candidates?**
Some travel expenses may be covered. An honorarium of $200 is paid for speaking at both Sunday services (9:00 and 10:30).

**15. Any additional information, which you think, is important?**
Information available: 2010—2015 Strategic Plan; Sunday Program; Awareness Newsletter; Endowment brochure; Relaxation Headquarters and Retreat Center brochures.

In December, Rev. Mary put together a team of volunteers to collect shoes for the homeless. It grew into the Shoes for Souls program that continues to distribute shoes on the third Monday of the month next to the Hope Van, which provides medical attention to the homeless. This was followed shortly thereafter by Rev. Barbara Leger and Rev. Pam Sanchez and a team of volunteers cooking Food for Hope on the third Monday. The food is served to the homeless at the same time and place.

# 2013

Roger Gray presented two popular workshops on Body Language.

In February, Dr. James Golden and Leslie Golden presented a two-day retreat called "The Journey Home." Rev. Sharon Kennedy's ordination ceremony took place during the retreat, which was a very special moment for her since Dr. James was her teacher and Leslie a friend for many years.

Rev. Kay Stewart's ordination took place in a special ceremony on a Sunday morning during service. Her family was very touched by the honoring of Rev. Kay's ministry.

The Center purchased an evening at Riverfront Playhouse for the show "Leading Ladies."

Jim and Julie Nelson invited the congregation to their home for a special daffodil social, when their thousands of daffodil bulbs were in bloom. Sandy Babcock and friends, whose band, Acoustic Summer, provided fresh and delightful music for the event.

The Endowment Committee made $4,497 available from the investment interest for special projects in the Center. The projects included:
- Source Group youth game development
- audio equipment for the Sound Team
- CD player for the pavilion
- sunscreen window covering for the sanctuary windows
- a hedge trimmer for the Landscape Team
- replacement tile and trim for the foyer

Dr. M. Hari Haaren visited from India and presented his workshop, "Sound Healing," a listening therapy program using specially filtered, classical Indian music to improve ear and brain function.

The Youth Group creatively sewed a wide assortment of small pillows for sale in the bookstore as a fundraiser for camp.

Phoebe Fazio offered classes "Toning on Tuesdays," using tone as a healing practice.

Local Buddhist teacher, Chris Carrigan, offered a popular five-week class on "The Four Foundations of Mindfulness" in the meditation pavilion.

In honor of the Foundations Class, Barbie Seiser contributed a magnificent gift to the Center, the adoption of an orphaned elephant named Lemoyian, which is cared for by the David Sheldrick Wildlife Trust in Africa.

*Adopted Orphan Elephant, Lemoyian*

A special fundraiser, Nourishing Our Community, was organized with volunteers who offered to host a special lunch or dinner, hike or other event, and the congregation bid on the limited spaces to attend the wide variety of options. It was very popular. Feasts included a pool party, patio boat sunset cruise on Lake Shasta, a Thoreau Saunter at Castle Crags, and many more. Over $5,000 was raised in this program and the responses from all who participated were terrific.

Bob Rock presented a four-week series on "What Lies Beneath the Surface," on the esotericism of world religions.

By July, the Minister Search Committee had reviewed 18 applicants for the Senior Minister position, held many interviews, and narrowed the field to the top two candidates, who spoke at Sunday services in

July. The members voted at a congregational meeting on August 11th, and one candidate received 76% of the vote, but then turned down the offer. The Board of Trustees agreed to "push the pause button" on the search for a new senior minister for a few months to reflect on the time and process used for the search.

The new agreement signed between the Board of Trustees and the Minister Selection Committee in November agreed to approach the search for a senior minister through a networking process instead of posting on the CSL headquarters website. Due to other commitments Traci Roberti and Fred Erickson could not continue on the committee. Robert Patari and Michael Bordeaux accepted the committee's invitation to fill those positions.

Dr. Kenn Gordon, Spiritual Leader of Centers for Spiritual Living, visited the Center and presented a powerful message and workshop about the vision of the organization.

Meetings began for those members and friends who planned a trip to Peru, called "Mystical Quest to Peru." Yoga teacher Donna Jackson, who is an expert on the culture and language of that area, led the planning for the adventure to take place in April 2014.

Rev. Dr. Kim Kaiser was a special guest speaker in October. Dr. Kim, Director of Education at the Center for Spiritual Living in Santa Rosa is also Academic and Regional Dean for the Holmes Institute School of Consciousness Studies. He was an ordained priest in the Soto School of Zen Buddhism as well as a minister of Religious Science.

Jo-Ann Rosen, ordained in the Tiep Hein Order in the Plum Village Tradition by Zen Master Thich Nhat Hanh, presented a Mindfulness Retreat called "Applied Ethics: Ground for the Spiritual Life."

Rev. Pam Sanchez repeated her popular class on "The Presence Process" based on the book by Michael Brown that included practical approaches to finding inner peace.

The Woman's Retreat, led by Rev. Sue, was sold out and took place at Coram Ranch near Lake Shasta. Sylvia Kunz was the main chef for the event.

The Center bought out the Riverfront Playhouse one evening for congregants to enjoy the play, "A Little Murder Never Hurt Any Body."

The Men's Group had its first retreat called "Awakening Sacred Masculine Energy," guided by Mark Telles, Hepwa Creek Men's Council, Brian Zanze of the Mankind Project, and Roy Woolfstead.

# 2014

In January, the congregation honored Dr. James Golden with a plaque that hangs on the meditation pavilion to honor his inspiration and vision in the development and construction of the pavilion.

Rev. Dr. Kim Kaiser began offering a class one Saturday a month, starting in February, on "Mysticism in World Religions." The first class was "Mysticism and Buddhism."

Special guest speaker, Rev. David Robinson from Clarkston, Washington, spoke on January 12th and presented a very popular workshop called "Lessons from Hogwarts School of Witchcraft and Wizardry."

Rev. Sharon Dunn, a staff minister at the Oakland Center for Spiritual Living, was a special guest speaker in February and presented a workshop on "The Science of Science of Mind."

The Endowment Committee announced $6,400 would be available from their investment interest for special projects in the Center.

At the January 27th board meeting, the Minister Selection Committee unanimously recommended to the board that candidate Rev. David Robinson would best fulfill the criteria for the position of Senior Minister. From all of their interviews, reference checks, questions and answers, and the experience of the congregation when Rev. David visited January 12th, the committee unanimously felt he was an outstanding candidate for the Senior Minister position.

The Board reviewed the documentation and reports of the committee and unanimously voted to invite Rev. David back to speak on Sunday, February 16th, to give members and opportunity to get to know him better, followed by a vote at the Annual Congregational Meeting on Sunday, March 9th.

Rev. David had been the senior minister at the Center for Spiritual Living, Lewis Clark Valley, in Clarkston, Washington, since April 2011.

Prior to that, he was a staff minister at the Center for Spiritual Living in Roseburg, Oregon for six months. Rev. David was licensed as a Practitioner at the Seattle Center for Spiritual Living in 2004. He entered The Holmes Institute for ministerial training in 2006 and graduated with a Master's Degree in Consciousness Studies, then licensed as a minister in 2010.

At the congregational meeting, Rev. David received 98% "yes" vote, much to the delight of everyone. He took the helm at the Center on April 7, 2014.

*Rev. David Robinson*

Special events planned for the balance of the year include:
- "Something More: Inspirations of the Heart and Soul" interactive concert with Jaia Lee, which will include music, poetry, dance, inspiration, and healing.
- "Mastery of Heart and Soul" workshop with Michael Dove where the heart will be explored physiologically, historically, and personally, so that soul level of truth will be revealed.
- May Day: A Joyful Flowering of the Feminine," a celebration with Alexa Singer-Telles and Maya Spector, using story, ritual, creative process, and the making of a soul collage.

- "Summer Solstice Celebration" at Whiskeytown. The congregation will enjoy a day of swimming, kayaking, lounging, and fun including a potluck dinner.
- Twenty-six people were registered to go on the Mystical Quest to Peru.
- Nourishing Our Community for 2014.

Rev. Sue and Rev. Mary resumed their previous positions as Assistant Ministers. The future of the Center for Spiritual Living, Redding is bright and with its dedicated Board, minister, practitioners, members, and friends, it has a solid base on which to thrive.

# APPENDIX

# LIST OF PHOTOS

| Image # | Caption |
|---------|---------|
| 1 | Harry Magill |
| 2 | Dr. Stephen Zukor |
| 3 | Rev. Wilma Burtsell |
| 4 | Rev. James Golden |
| 5 | Sherry Miller |
| 6a | Sue Miller at Camp Latieze |
| 6b | Fun at Camp |
| 6c | Chris Johnson at Camp |
| 6d | Workshops at Camp |
| 7a | Teens relax at Camp Latieze |
| 7b | Odd Games at Camp |
| 7c | The Grape Test at Camp |
| 8a | Building under Construction |
| 8b | Construction of the Sanctuary |
| 8c | Skeleton Completed |
| 8d | Phase One Completed |
| 9 | Half Dome Hike for Youth |
| 10 | Half Dome Hike |
| 11 | Celebration of Rev. James |
| 12a | Murder Mystery Party Investigation |
| 12b | Youth serving the Party |
| 12c | The Suspicious Stewart Family |
| 13 | James and Andrea |
| 14 | Golden Family |
| 15 | Meditation Pavilion Construction |
| 16 | Skydiving Adventure |

## Graphics:
## Graphic #    Description

# KEY EVENTS BY YEAR

**YEAR** **EVENT**

**1978** "The Body Alive" class with Janice Carrico
A letter was sent to headquarters requesting Harry be appointed the Associate Minister of Administration
A Halloween party was held at the Redding Grange Hall
A luau was held with dancing to Floyd Fowler's orchestra
A rubber raft and boat motor were raffled as a fundraiser

**1979** Dr. Zukor offered a 3-week course on "The Steps to Consciousness"
Steven LeVelle presented a workshop
St. Patrick's Day Dinner and Dance at Pacheco School
Ice Cream and Pie Social for singles also at the school
Dr. Zukor's radio show received many responses to the broadcast
Dr. Zukor's summer class was "Mystic Path to Cosmic Power"

**1980** A "Prosperity Seminar" was presented by Rev. Rosaline Hockett

**1981** Rev. Jay Scott Neale presented a seminar
Rev. Richard Green presented "Winning at the Game of Life Seminar"

**1982** Progressive dinner party
Halloween Party

Harvest Dinner at Bridge Bay Resort
Festival of Light held at the Redding Women's Club

1983    Roy Eugene Davis presented a seminar at the Shasta Inn.
St. Patrick's Day potluck
Wedding Vow Renewal Ceremony
A Talent Show was held at the Women's Club
Church Retreat at Camp Latieze
Church Barbeque at the Oak Mesa property
Rev. Tom Johnson was guest speaker for the Harvest Dinner at Bridge Bay Resort

1985    The board hired Pat Gage as Administrative Assistant for $100/month.
Marilyn Wray volunteered to be bookkeeper
"Love and Nature" workshop
Harvest Dinner at the Lorenz Hotel
Camp Latieze fall family retreat
Ten Zen Telles Seminar

1986    "Right Livelihood" Seminar
The board released Blanche from her commitment to play the organ at services and opened up opportunities for musicians in the community to play
Camp Latieze Couples Retreat
White water raft trip
Dr. Kennedy Schultz to speak at the November Harvest Dinner
Andrea Golden's Retreat Cookbook Kickoff

1987    Holistic Health Faire
Shakespeare Festival Trip
"Meditation, Visualization & Embodiment Seminar" by Dr. Richard Green
Fall Family Retreat
"Relationship Seminar" by Dr. Arleen Bump
Guest Speaker, Bob Trask

Alpha Awareness Training by Wally Minto
"Understanding Relationships" by Wally Minto
Monday morning breakfasts with Practitioners at the Park Marina Restaurant
Annual Arts and Craft Faire

**1988**    Easter Sunrise Service
Bob Trask presented "The Natural Way to Wealth Seminar"
Dr. Richard Green presented a seminar of "Meditation, Visualization and Embodiment."
Fall Family Retreat
Hosted the beer and food booth at the Boat Show as a fundraiser
White Water Raft Trip on the Klamath River
Hosted a Tandori Chicken food booth at the Old Shasta Art Festival as a fundraiser
Children participated in the International Children's Art Network Project
Andrea Golden became a Reverend at a celebration ceremony on June 24
The church leased space at 1109 Hartnell, Suite 9 for an office and bookstore
New location for Sunday Services at the Sierra Room at the Red Lion Hotel or the Holiday Inn
Charlie and Lori Thweatt presented a concert
Wedding Vows Renewal Ceremony
Sexuality Seminar: "The Male-Female Relationship"
Rev. James began a weekly 1/2 hour TV program on Cable TV called "Principles for Successful Living"
Barry and Joyce Vissell presented "The Spiritualized Relationship Seminar"
A couples retreat was held in Ashland, Oregon
Brian O'Leary, Ph.D. and former astronaut presented a seminar on "Exploring Inner and Outer Space"
Harvest Dinner held at Junell's Restaurant at Gold Hills Country Club
"Musical Seminar" by Maxine Colbert

**1989** "Getting to Know You Workshop" with Maxine Kaye Nielsen

"Exploring Total Human Potential Seminar" with Dr. Bill Little

"Work is Love Made Visible" by Rev. James Golden

Locations for Sunday Service include Shasta College Amphitheater and the Shasta Inn

Women's retreat in Trinidad

"Introduction into Skydiving" with Rev. James

"How to Fall in Love Again" with Rev. James

"Life is Risky Business" with Rev. James

Cajun Progressive Dinner

"Money is God in Action" with Rev. James Golden

Church Family Reunion at Anderson River Park

Labor Day Family Retreat

**1990** "Science, Spirit, and You Workshop" by Dr. Brian O'Leary

"Community Open House and Concert" with Charlie and Lori Thweat

Couple's retreat in Healdsberg, CA

White water raft trip on the Rogue River

"The Midas Touch Seminar" with Rev. James Golden

Concert by pianist, Machiko Kobialka and violinist Daniel Kobialka

Half Dome Club, 8-day backpacking trip for Junior Youth Group to Yosemite

"How to Breakthrough into Unlimited Success and Prosperity Seminar" by Dr. Frank Richelieu

The StorySingers in Concert

"Common Sense Spirituality" with Bob Trask

Celebratory roast in honor of Rev. James' 10th year in ministry

Bus trip to Medford to hear Ram Dass speak

Annual church picnic

"How to Fall in Love Again Workshop" with Rev. James and Rev. Andrea

"Church Family Retreat" at Camp Latieze

"Principles for Successful Living" Workshops
"Parenting with Crazy Wisdom" Workshops
"Life, You Wanna Make Something of It?" with Dr. Tom Costa
All American Chili Cook Off
Celebration Harvest Dinner and Dance
"Seminar for People Who do Too Much" with Rev. Andrea
Unexpected Income Program

1992 Book signing celebration, *Jump Into Life with Rev. James Golden* by Mary Schroeder
"Marinara and Mayhem, Pasta and Pavarotti All Star Spaghetti Feed and Variety Show"
Dr. James Horton's workshop on "Building Relationships"
"The Thrill of Skydiving" with Rev. James
Mary Schroeder and Paul Mitchell lead a new singles group
Rev. Dr. Carleton Whitehead seminar
Dr. Earlene Castellaw, RSI Field Service Representative, presented a class to the SOM IV students
"Windows to the Soul" music concert by Tienne Beaulieu
Prayers and Blessings Meditation Retreat
"Parenting with Love and Logic" with Dr. Andrea and Francie Parr
Cross Country Ski Trip
"Progressive Dinner and Concert" by Rick Copeland, Charlie Nimovitz, Electric Shakti and Heartsangha Choir
Committed Couples Retreat
Western BBQ and Dance

1993 Jaine Ryder-Howard's minister licensing and celebration as Staff Minister
Rev. Andrea's ordination ceremony
Celebration for Administrator, Rev. Jeffrey Proctor, who accepted a pastor position in Knoxville, Tennessee
RCRS Cookbook Project
Mid-week healing services during July
Rev. David Leonard spoke on "Spirit Wants to Dance"

"Music of the Spheres" with Dr. Robert Bowman and John Creighton-Murray
Singles Retreat in Medford Oregon
Halloween Party and Costume Parade
Chagdud Tulku Rinpoche presented a talk
Christmas In July workshop on creating crafts
Cowboy Barbeque and Reader's Theatre Night

**1994**   Rev. James elected to Religious Science International Board, heading Credentials and Placement
Program by His Holiness Kusum Lingpa
"Summer Memories Benefit Concert" by Rick Copeland
"Speaking From the Heart Seminar" by Rev. James Turrell
Concert by Emam and Bruce Hamm
"Song and Celebration Concert" by Kirtana
"Guess Who's Coming to Dinner" Mystery Get Together
White Water Raft Trip
Cottage is purchased and set up on site, open for children's church
Head Start remodels the cottage and leases it for school
Shakespeare Theater trip to Ashland to see "Much Ado About Nothing"
Family Retreat at Camp Latieze
Singles Retreat in Ashland, Oregon
Doctorate Ceremony for Dr. James
Dr. John McMurphy presented the "Myth and Our Search for Truth Seminar"
Craft Bazaar
Winter Solstice Event
Last meeting of the Singles Group that met for two years
Benefit Concert with Electric Shakti performing
Children's Christmas Tea and Theatrical Production
Christmas Day (Sunday) noon service

**1995**   Begin two Sunday services at 9:00 and 10:30
Charlie Thweatt Concert

Benefit Concert with John Creighton-Murray, Dr. Robert Bowman and Leslie Lundberg

Annual Church Picnic in Anderson River Park with the Electric Shakti Band

Bob Mills, master woodwind player

Meditation Retreat

Bus trip to Ashland, Oregon to attend "Macbeth" at the Shakespeare Theater

Dr. Robert Bowman Concert

Practitioner Mary Schroeder elected as lay person to RSI Board of Directors

Week-by-Week Summer Camp for 5-10 year olds

"Parenting Solutions Program" by Dr. James and Rev. Andrea

Rev. Sandra Rudh installed at Mt. Shasta Church and received church charter status

"Longing to Know Workshop" by Pamela White and Cheryl Williams

Junior Youth Camp Out and Rafting Adventure at Castle Crags

Jr. Youth Big Lagoon Annual Camp Out

Labor Day Retreat at Camp Latieze with Charlie Thweat

Rev. Jaine Ryder-Howard's installation as pastor of the Contra Costa Church

Rev. Frankie Timmers Workshop

Toni Thomas and Joe Niemiec's Wedding

"Light of Seva" Team Potluck and Rally

Practitioner Practicum

Dr. James and Rev. Andrea celebrate their twentieth wedding anniversary

**1996**  Grand opening of the Meditation Pavilion with mini-meditation retreat

"Talent Show and Spaghetti Feed" with the Youth Group

All night chant with Dr. James Golden

The stained glass project began, supported by memorial contributions

Dr. James chosen as a chaplain for the Redding Police Department

Dr. James to serve on the Chaplaincy Advisory Board at Redding Medical Center

Chico Religious Science Church Choir Performance

"Parenting with Love and Logic" by Gerri Brousseau and Lauri Gibson

Rev. Jaine Ryder-Howard Seminar, "Celebration!"

Charlie Thweat Concert

An Old Fashioned Church Picnic in Caldwell Park

Meditation Retreat: "The Heart is the Hub of All Sacred Spaces"

Bus trip to San Francisco to see Deepak Chopra

"Life is Risky Business Seminar" followed by skydiving with Dr. James

Church Picnic in Caldwell Park

"Choose Prosperity Now!" Seminar with JD Hunt, Paul Mitchell and Mary Schroeder

"Spiritual Practices with Heart" Seminar by Carol Chase-Rapin, Kay Stewart, Leslie Gilbertie, and Pam Sanchez

Dr. John McMurphy "Seminar on Living Deliberately"

Love Is… Couples Retreat in Arcata

Church trip to Disneyland

"Debt Free and Prosperous Living Seminar" by Michael Bordeaux

Harvest Dinner theme was "Puttin' on the Ritz"

"Cowboy BQ and Poetry Reading"

Labor Day Retreat at Camp Latieze, "Wherever You Go, There You Are!"

"Children's Christmas Tea Party" held by the Youth Group

Home and Heart Bazaar

Christmas Cookie Exchange

1997    "Poem Crazy!" Event

"Finding Your Way Back Home Seminar" with Dr. Jonathan Young

Wilderness Adventure (camping and solo treks)

Summer Affinity Groups, small group workshops
"Love and Logic" Parenting Classes
"Debt Free and Prosperous Living Seminar"
Dr. John Orlando Piano Recital
The Mysterious Disappearance of Al Capone, a murder mystery party
Youth Group Camp Out at Castle Crags
Will and Estate Seminar
Synaptic Gap trio from Knoxville in concert
Klamath River white water rafting trip
Interfaith Softball League
BBQ and Country Line Dancing Party
Theme for the Harvest Dinner: "Indiana James and the Temple of Light"
David Ault, composer and song writer, performed
Annual CROP Walk Fundraiser to benefit local food banks

1998    The bell for the sanctuary was purchased and paid for in one day
Permit application for a new wing off the sanctuary was submitted to the City
Bank loan was refinanced at $575,000
"Nasrudin Seminar" with Dr. James Golden
"The Mystical Journey of Carl Jung, Forever Jung" by John Maxwell Taylor
"Secrets of Sociological Aikido, The Invisible Art of Spiritual Self Defense" with John Maxwell Taylor
Rick Copeland in Concert
"Inspiring the Senses Seminar" with Shelli Compton-Orser, owner of Trinity Essential Oils
Affinity Groups met during the summer
Chocolate Lovers' Book Fair
"Advanced Directives Seminar" with Dr. Bruce Bartlow
Love and Logic Parenting Classes with Rev. Andrea
Aryeh David In Concert
"Putting Relate back into Relationships" with Dr. Bill Taliaferro

"Communion: Deepening Spiritual Focus Workshop" by Kathy Zavada

A Meditation Retreat at Camp Latieze: "Gratitude, A Path With Joy"

Don Ericson Piano Concert

Swami Beyondananda, Steve Bhaerman, presented an inspiring live performance

Wilderness Adventure at Mt. Shasta

"The Power of the Focused Heart Workshop" with Charley Thweatt

"I Am Spirit" concert by Charley Thweatt

Country BBQ and Bake Off event

A bus trip to Ashland to see the Shakespeare play Cymbeline

Labor Day Family Retreat at Camp Latieze

"Mystical Power of Music Seminar" with Dyveke Spino

"Drawing from the Heart Seminar" with Bobbie Phillips-Copeland

"Shifting into Miracle Thinking Seminar" with Dr. James

Children's Christmas Tea Party presented by the Source Youth Group

**1999**   Progressive Dinner

Dennis Steinke and the "Thunderbolt Meditation Seminar"

Installation of Rev. Alice Carpenter as Staff Minister

Easter Sunrise service

Spring Meditation Experience called "Entering The Silence"

Kathy Zavada Concert

Patty Bay Seminar on "alming Down, Clearing Out"

"Thank God I Am Rich! Seminar" with Dr. Dennis Merritt Jones

Shelli Rizzi's "Urban Shamanism" on aromatherapy and ritual

Celebration to open the new wing on Saturday, June 26

Mt. Lassen Moonlight Hike

Riverfront Playhouse performance "Nunsense II" starring church member, Jennifer Levens

Moved James' office into the new wing of the church

Tibetan Monks Program
Patty Bay Seminar
James Turrell Seminar
Couple's Retreat
Chocolate Lover's Art & Book Faire

**2000** Celebration for Rev. Carol Chase's move to Santa Rosa
Women's Retreat
Mary Manin Morrissey Seminar, "Building Your Field of Dreams"
Kathy Zavada Workshop for the Music Department
Kelly Carter, Administrative Assistant moves to Oregon
Michael and Justine Toms seminar, from New Dimensions Public Radio
Church Retreat at Camp Latieze with Kathy Zavada
Redding Medical Center begins Chaplain Program, 5 practitioners attend
Dr. Carolyn McKeown guest speaker
"God At 2000" Video Series from the Oregon State University Symposium
RSI leaders Dr. Kennedy Shultz and Dr. Carlton Whitehead make their transition
Trinity River Rafting Adventure
Daniel Nahmod in concert
"Bookstore Water Project" for a community water tank in Africa
Dessert Lovers' Book and Art Faire
Meditation Seminar
Don Miguel Ruiz Program
Dr. James receives the Ernest Holmes Award at the RSI Conference
"Life is Risky Business & Cross Country Skiing" with Dr. James
Caribbean Windjammer Cruise with snorkel lessons by Chris Hooykaas
A fall Progressive Dinner
A Spaghetti Feed and Talent Show

"Murder at Midnight," New Year's Eve Murder Mystery Party

2001    Gaden Shartse Tibetan Monks Visit and Perform
Grey Levay Workshop
Committed Couples Weekend in Trinidad
Wedding Vow Renewal Ceremony
Inter-Faith Dialogue
Tienne Beaulieu special benefit concert
"Teachings on Love," a mindfulness retreat with Dharmacharya Lyn Fine
Patty Bay workshop on "Healthy Relationships" using her book *Therapy in a Nutshell*
Wilderness Experience at Butte Lake in Lassen Park
Labor Day Retreat at Camp Latieze
Cornerstone Chorale and Brass presented a "Sacred Music Concert"

2002    Family Retreat at Camp Latieze on Origins of the Heart
Patrick's Point Annual Campout
Anton Mizerak Concert
Swami Vasudev Program and Workshop
Terry Cole-Whittaker talk and seminar on her book *Every Saint has a Past, Every Sinner a Future*
Wilderness Adventure on Antelope Creek
First Poker Run and Picnic
Melissa Phillippe presented Sunday talks and a concert
Holiday Concert with Kathy Zavada
AIDS Memorial Service

2003    Practitioner shawls purchased
Doug Von Koss Music Workshop
Anton & Friends in Concert
"The Peace Walker Society" event
Talent Show and Spaghetti Feed
Alan Cohen presented his "Living Juicy Seminar"

Meditation Retreat, "Abide in Love"
Spiritual Parenting Group
Rev. Andrea elected to Religious Science International Board of Directors
First Endowment Regatta at the Woolfsteads
Drum Journey with Joe Niemiec
Family Picnic at Kid's Kingdom
Couples Class
Freddie Weber Music Concert and Workshop
Nasrudin Bazaar
Church name change to Spiritual Enrichment Center
Spiritual Community Directory published
North State Youth Group Lock-in
Rev. David Ault, "Where Regret Cannot Find Me Workshop"
Community Retreat in McCloud

2004    Coyote Men's Circle
First meeting of Wisdom Keepers by Rev. Sue MillerBorn
"Clearing Your Life with Feng Shui" with Nancy Pernell and Dr. Andrea
Hepwa Creek Men's Council Gatherings
Spiritual Parenting Group
Spiritual Singles Meeting on the book *If the Buddha Dated*
Spiritual Community Practice Center Gatherings
Fr. Leo Booth workshop on the "Five Spiritual Laws of Ancient Wisdom"
"Starting Over Single" class with Mike Jones and Dr. Andrea
"Snowshoe Walk for Peace" with Rev. Sue
Roy Eugene Davis workshop on "Meditation and God Realization"
Booth at Relay for Life
Benji Wertheimer and Shiva Divas in concert
"Spirit in Recovery" meetings with Rev. Joe Niemiec
Endowment Regatta
"Mindfulness Retreat" at Whiskeytown with Buddhist teachers Larry and Peggy Ward

Dinner and Talent Show
"Forgiveness Seminar" with Dr. Andrea and Rev. Sue Miller
"40 Days to Transformation" summer program
"Women's Self-Defense and Healing Workshop" with Paul Davis
Women's Retreat on "The Feminine Face of God"
"Paddle and Picnic for Peace" at Castle Lake
Whitewater Rafting Trip on the Lower Klamath River
"Cultivating the Satisfied Heart Retreat" with River Oaks Sangha
"The Energy of Money Seminar" with Maria Nemeth
"An Evening of Poetry and a Day of Magic" with Doug von Koss
"Options to Anger Workshop" with John Crumbley, Ph.D.
New Year's Eve Sapta

2005    "Creating a Spiritually Engaged Practice" by Dharmavidya David Brazier and Prasada Caroline Brazier
Parking Lot Sale
Regional practitioner meeting in Redding
"Snowshoe for Peace Walk" with Rev. Sue
Chicken Barbeque and Talent Show
"Men's Retreat with Doug von Koss and John Robinson
"Free the Heart Seminar" with David Jones
Adopt a Soldier Project
"Invoking the Sage Workshop" with Jonathan Young, Ph.D.
Mind, Body, Spirit Faire
"In the Midst of it All" Meditation Retreat
Shakespeare Trip to Ashland
A Season of Nonviolence, Profiles & Discussion
Marilyn Vondrachek donated all plants from Joe's memorial to the meditation garden
Endowment Regatta at the Mitchells
Rev. Dr. Andrea Golden and Joe Asebeso's wedding
Sunset Drum Group
Garden Shartse Tibetan Monks Tour

**2006**   Celebration of Rev. Pam Sanchez' Ordination
Rev. Dr. Candice Beckett, President of RSI visited and spoke
at both services
"Sound Healing Didgeridoo Concert" by Chris Neville
"Living the Life You Love Workshop" by Mary Manin
Morrissey
Karen Drucker in Concert
Ashland Sufi dancers for Universal Peace
Snowshoe for Peace
Mind, Body, Spirit Faire
Rogue River Raft Trip
"Poetry for Peace Social" for Season for Non-Violence
Peace walk on the Sundial Bridge
"Free the Heart Workshop" by David Jones
Joan Borysenko Workshop on "Wisdom of the Heart and
From Stress to Strength"
"Calming the Fearful Mind Mindfulness Retreat" with the
Nuns of Deer Park Monastery
Fall Women's Retreat in Ashland, Oregon
Open Heart Gathering and Potluck
Lt. Col. Dave Grossman Seminar on "Media Violence and
Violent Crime"
Annual Parking Lot Sale
The first Floating of the Lanterns event
Tienne Beaulieu received her practitioner license

**2007**   Announcement of Rev. Sue MillerBorn as Assistant Minister
Creation of the Health Ministry coordinated by Sandy
Babcock and Bonnie Lantiegne
Peter Kater in Concert
Rev. Joe and Rev. Toni Niemiec's Farewell Party
German Pianist Sontraud Speidel in Concert
"Restorative Yoga Workshop" presented by Silke Richmond,
Certified Ananda Yoga Teacher
"Workshop on Quantum Mechanics" by Dr. Amit Goswami
"Spring Meditation Retreat" at Camp Latieze

"Claiming our Stories Workshop" by Jonathan Young, Ph.D, Founding Curator of the Joseph Campbell Archives and Library

"Opening to Anxiety with Awareness and Compassion" by Bruce Tift, MA, LMFT

Empty Bowls Clay Workshops

Klamath River Raft Trip

"Day of Healing" organized by Sandy Babcock

"Healing with Love, Compassion and the Power of the Focused Mind" by Harold McCoy

"Finding Our Way Home, Moonlight Peace Paddle at Brandy Creek" by Rev. Sue MillerBorn

Stephen Pike, music intuitive and composer, presented his original music compositions

Mind, Body, Spirit Faire

Annual Parking Lot Sale

Annual Piggy Reunion by the Endowment Committee

"The Mystery of Purpose and Destiny Workshop" by Jean Houston

A Woman's Worth Retreat

"The Visionary Window: Integration of Science and Spirituality" by Dr. Amit Goswami

**2008**    Fundraiser to build the labyrinth: Bill Parr cycling cross country

"Living Your Passion: Life Purpose Here and Now Workshop" with Patrick Harbula

"Joy is All There Is Meditation Retreat" with Bill Martin

Regional Practitioner Meeting, theme The Gateway

"How Good Can It Get Workshop" with Alan Cohen

Gentle Thunder and Will Clipman Concert

"Dances of Universal Peace" by Yahya Ali Nadler and Raphael Birney

"Rumi: Love and the Spiritual Path", a Sufi Workshop by Raphael Birney, MD

"Healing Ministry - Preparing for Surgery" by Sandy Babcock, RN

Walk Around The World (monthly peace walks)
Piggy Reunion by the Endowment Committee
Ordination of Rev. Mary Mitchell
"The Enneagram of Relationship Workshop" with Carl Marsak
Mind, Body, Spirit Faire
Pastor Candidates Speak
Retirement Celebration for Dr. Andrea Asebedo
Welcome new pastors Rev. Judith Churchman and Rev. Bob Luckin
Floating of the Lanterns
"Saying Yes to Change: Essential Wisdom for Your Journey" by Joan Borysenko

**2009**    "Standing Firm when Your Whole World is Shaking" by Mary Manin Morrissey
"Name Your Year Seminar" with Rev. Judith Churchman and Rev. Bob Luckin
"Chants Encounter Concert and Spiritual Workshop" by Charley Thweatt
"Gandhi and the Teachings of the Gita" by Rev. Sue MillerBorn
Walk Around the World
"Inherit the Wind" a play by The Players
Booth at Relay for Life
"Clear the Clutter Workshop" with Lita Evans
"Emergency Preparedness" classes with Jim Nelson
"Lifting Your Spirits with Weights" with Willy McCarty
"The Star Power Workshop"
"Breath of Fresh Air Workshop" with Rev. Sue MillerBorn
Ashana in Concert
Bioneers Class
"Raw Food Miracle Seminar" with Tonya Zavasta
The Players present "Harvey"
Namaste Café
"Exceptional Living Workshop" with Rev. Lynn Fritz
Burney Peace Walk

Lema Ranch Walks with Gwen Knaebel
"Reiki I Workshop" with Vicki Lawrence
Phil Aldrich Memorial Walk
"Suggestion and the Art of Influence Seminar" with Roger Gray
Summer Solstice Barbeque and Square Dance
Lower Klamath River Rafting Trip
Pet Blessing Ceremony
Men's Retreat with Doug von Koss
Barbeque and Petting Zoo at the Kramerman and McCarty home
Snowshoe for Peace Walk
"Dancing the Spiral" Woman's Retreat
"The Power of I Am" by John Maxwell Taylor
"A Musing Musical Mystic Concert" by Grey Tamblyn
"A Bowl of Soup & a Song," an evening with the Rolling Crones
"Raw Food Miracle: Make Aging an Option" by Tonya Zavasta
"Transformational Healing Music" with Anton Mizerak and Kim Lorene
Healing Arts Cottage Grand Opening
Parking Lot Sale
"Full Moon Picnic Paddle" at Whiskeytown Lake
Mind, Body, Spirit Faire
"Heal Your Life, Rewrite Your Life's Story Workshop" with Rev. Bob Luckin
Art Hop at CSL
"Living Healthy" class with Tienne Beaulieu
"Diving Into the Divine" by Dr. Dennis Merritt Jones
"Holiday Mandala Workshop" with Rev. Bob Luckin
"A Soul Work Retreat" with Rod Raphael Birney and Yahya Suzanna Nadler
The Players present "It's a Wonderful Life"

**2010**    Wedding Vows Renewal
"You and Your Desires Workshop" by Terry McBride

Labyrinth Dedication to Dr. Andrea Asebedo

"Grace, Ease, and Joy Mini Retreat" with Rev. Sharon Kennedy

"Heart of a Woman," Women's Retreat

Booth at Relay for Life

The Players present "The Dining Room" stage play

"Finding Your Way Home Seminar" with Jonathan Young, Ph.D.

Peace, Love and CSLR Goods & Services Auction

"The God Dialogue" with Rod Loomis and Rev. Sandy Freeman Loomis

New Visioning Meetings

Tienne Beaulieu named choir director at All Saint's Episcopal Church

Family Campout at Patrick's Point

Strategic Plan 2010-2015 completed

"Renewing Love's Spark" with Rev. Bob Luckin

Ballroom Dancing Lessons with Laurie Hallum

"Constructive Conflict Resolution Seminar" with Dr. Patty Bay

"Creativity, Letting Go and Life Workshop" with Jodee Merrill

Maria Nemeth Workshop

"Being Me and Loving You Workshop" with Kelly Bryson, MFT

"Handwriting Analysis Workshop" with Bob Luckin

"Be Smart with your Money Workshop" with Lorna McLeod

"Learning to Receive Your Divine Guidance" with Bobbie G and Roger Gray

Object D'Art Silent Auction

"Better Living through Living Foods Workshop" with Jaia Lee

Jonas Magram Concert

"Mandala Workshop" with Bob Luckin

Ticket and a Tile Fundraiser for a new roof on the sanctuary

Soup and Spirit Readings

"Experience the Power of the Mastermind" with Lynne Imel

Candlelight Concert with Holly Day
"Pirates of Penzance Play" by Shasta College
"The Big Energy Gamble" panel discussion
"The Tao of Forgiveness Workshop" with William Martin
Namaste Café
"Organic Gardening" with Linda Aldrich
"Spiritual Cooking" with Sylvia Kunz and Dr. Andrea
Spiritual Thanksgiving with Dinner & Games
Holiday Silent Goods & Services Auction and Craft Faire
"Commit to Your Dreams Workshop" with Bob Luckin
New Year's Rockin' Eve Potluck, Dinner & Dance

**2011**    "2012 and Beyond: Lighten Up!" by Mellen-Thomas Benedict
Congregational Survey completed
Seva Appreciation Dinner
"Lend Me a Tenor" play at Riverfront Playhouse
"Prosperity Plus Workshop" with Rev. Edwene Gaines
Gaden Shartse Monks present "Sacred Earth Healing Arts
of Tibet"
"The Power of the Present: Beyond the Prodigal Path" by
Rev. Gary Layman
"The Art and Practice of Living with Nothing and No One
Against You" by Gary Simmons, Ph.D.
Going Away Party for Ace Clemens and Erin Szymanski
Namaste Café
Rev. Sue MillerBorn's ordination
Rev. Lynn Fritz's ordination
Ace Clemens to Malawi, Africa with youth to build a school

**2012**    "Vendanta Yoga: The Source Wisdom of Oneness" by Dave
DeLuca
"The Q Effect" by Gary Simmons, Ph.D
Plants and Treasures Sale
"The Presence Process" with Rev. Pam Sanchez
"Mystic Mondays" with Rev. Sue MillerBorn
Patrick's Point Campout

"Taking Control of Your Creative Mind Workshop" by Terry McBride

Retirement party for Rev. Bob and Rev. Judith

Interim Co-Pastors, Rev. Sue MillerBorn and Rev. Mary Mitchell

Booth at the Chamber of Commerce Business Expo featuring the Center as "Your Stress Reduction Headquarters"

"Co-Creation Workshops" with Rev. Eileen Brownell

"Complete vs. Finished Workshops" with Rev. Sue, Rev. Mary, and Phoebe Fazio

"In the Quietness of the Soul," a Retreat for Women at Ananda Retreat Center

Shoes for Souls Program began distributing used shoes to the homeless

**2013**    "The Journey Home Retreat" with Dr. James Golden and Leslie Golden

Ordination Ceremonies for Rev. Sharon Kennedy and Rev. Kay Stewart

"Leading Ladies" play at the Riverfront Playhouse

"Four Foundations of Mindfulness" with Chris Carrigan

World Labyrinth Day walk

"Body Language Workshop" with Roger Gray

"Daffodil Delight" at the Nelson's Home

"Mini Urban Retreat" with Rev. Sharon Kennedy and Tara Steele

Family Camping Trip to Patrick's Point

"Toning on Tuesdays" with Phoebe Fazio

Food for Hope Program began

Foundations Class adopts Lemoyian, an orphan elephant through Sheldrick Wildlife Trust

"Nourishing Our Community," a Feast, Fellowship and Friends Event

"Esoterics - What Lies Beneath the Surface" with Robert Rock

"Building a Healthcare Team" with Karen Coffey and Rev. Sharon Kennedy

"Paths to Wellness Workshop" with Leslie Powers

"Sacred Chants and Healings Powers of Indian Music Therapy" with Dr. M. Hari Haaren

"Living in the Light Women's Retreat" at Coram Ranch with Rev. Sue MillerBorn

"Transformational Music and Sacred Chants" with Anton Mizerak and Laura Berryhill

Visit by Dr. Kenn Gordon, Spiritual Leader of Centers for Spiritual Living

"Make Me an Instrument of Thy Peace" class with Rev. Barbara Leger

Congregational vote for a new senior minister

Jo-ann Rosen presented a workshop in "Applied Ethics: Ground for the Spiritual Life"

Workshop on "The Tao" by Rev. Dr. Kim Kaiser, also a guest speaker

"A Little Murder Never Hurt Anybody" at Riverfront Playhouse

"Getting Comfortable with Investing" with Deb Black

Special guest speaker, Rev. Heather Hennessey

2014    Visioning Core began meeting the first Sunday of the month

Rev. David Robinson spoke and held a workshop on "Hogwart's School of Witchcraft & Wizardry"

"What are You Hungry For?" a class offered by Cher Matthews

"Finding Happiness" at Friday Night at the Movies

Youth Group held a Bunco Game

"Removing Barriers to Financial Success" by Rev. Barbara Leger

"A Course in Miracles" weekly class offered by Diana Johnson

Rev. Dr. Kim Kaiser's monthly class on "Mysticism and World Religions"

Guest speaker Rev. Sharon Dunn who presented a workshop on "The Science in Science of Mind"

Guest speaker Rev. Georgia Prescott, CSL Sacramento

CSL Sacramento's theater group presented "Authentic Voices"

Seva Rally to engage more people in selfless service to God through Seva Teams

"Something More: Inspirations of the Heart and Soul" with Jaia Lee

"Mastery of Heart and Soul" with Michael Dove, also a guest speaker

Guest Speaker Chris Carrigan

Rev. David Robinson voted to be Senior Pastor of CSL Redding

## Board of Trustees by Year
## (after vote at Congregational
## Meeting)

**1978**
Don Churchill, President
Bille Sue Dethlefs
Ed Ewing
Marlene Herrin
Dorothy Johnson
Harry Magill
Chris Maxwell
Bill Seifert
Dr. Stephen Zukor

**1979**
Harry Magill, Pres.
Bille Sue Dethlefs
Ed Ewing
Marlene Herrin
Bob Huntoon
Alice Scarbrough
Bill Seiffert
Dr. Stephen Zukor

**1980**
Don Churchill, President
Rev. Wilma Burtsell
Bille Sue Dethlefs
Ed Ewing
Bruce Johnson
Harry Magill
Alice Scarbrough
Bill Seiffert

**1981**
Don Churchill, President
Marge Benner

Rev. Wilma Burtsell
Billie Sue Dethlefs
Fred Erickson
Pat Gage
Bruce Johnson
Bill Seiffert
Dave Waterhouse

**1982**
Rev. James Golden, Pres.
Colleen Arendall
Billie Sue Dethlefs
Fred Erickson
Alice Holley
Emily Hylton
Ed Lawsom
Vic Panks
Carol Whetstone
Hal Wooten

**1983**
Rev. James Golden, Pres.
Don Churchill
Fred Erickson
Ed Ewing
Alice Holly
Ed Lawson
Judy Sanders
Billie Stutts White
Hal Wootton

**1985**
Rev. James Golden, Pres.
Fred Erickson
Ed Ewing
Pat Gage
Chuck Hancock
Marlene Herrin

Kathy Hooykaas
Bob Huntoon
Sherry Miller

1986
Rev. James Golden, Pres.
Chuck Hancock
Marlene Herrin
Cathy Hooykaas
Chris Hooykaas
Lee Houser
Bob Huntoon
Sherry Miller
Hal Muns

1987
Rev. James Golden, Pres.
Leslie Gilbertie
Chuck Hancock
Chris Hooykaas
Julia Houser
Bob Huntoon
Sherry Miller
Beverly Source
Lucille Tyner

1988
Rev. James Golden, Pres.
Hunter DeMarais
Lewanna Eskew
Leslie Gilbertie
Julia Houser
Bob Huntoon
Beverly Sorce
Lucille Tyner

1989
Rev. James Golden, Pres.

Frances Bleile
Leslie Gilbertie
Jaine Howard
Bob Huntoon
Bruce Johnson
Pat Kuehne
Lucille Tyner
Lewanna Wagner

1990
Rev. James Golden, Pres.
Frances Bleile
Phillip Clinger
Leslie Gilbertie
Jaine Howard
Pat Kuehne
Holly Moore
Mary Schroeder
Pat Yarbrough

1991
Rev. James Golden, Pres.
Frances Bleile
Leslie Gilbertie
Phillip Clinger
Jaine Howard
Pat Kuehne
Holly Moore
Mary Schroeder
Pat Yarbrough

1992
Rev. James Golden, Pres.
Frances Bleile
Philip Clinger
Jim Gilbertie
Pat Kuehne
Holly Moore

Mary Schroeder
Jan Ulrich
Pat Yarbrough

1993
Rev. James Golden, Pres.
Frances Bleile
Philip Clinger
Jim Gilbertie
Mark Ibsen
Sharon Kennedy
Holly Moore
Jaine Ryder-Howard
Jan Ulrich

1994
Rev. James Golden, Pres.
Jim Gilbertie
Sharon Kennedy
Teresa Lavagnino
Holly Moore
Mary Schroeder
Mike Stewart
Toni Thomas
Jan Ulrich

1995
Dr. James Golden, Pres.
Alice Carpenter
Debbie DeMarais
Sharon Kennedy
Teresa Lavagnino
Bev Sorce
Mike Stewart
Mary Schroeder
Toni Thomas
1996
Dr. James Golden, Pres.

Alice Carpenter
Carol Chase-Rapin
Debbie DeMarias
Teresa Lavagnino
Paul Mitchell
Pam Sanchez
Bev Source
Mike Stewart

1997
Dr. James Golden, Pres.
Alice Carpenter
Carol Chase-Rapin
Debbie DeMarais
Paul Mitchell
Joe Niemiec
Jill Ruesch
Pam Sanchez
Gary Solberg

1998
Dr. James Golden, Pres.
Dede Burk
Carol Chase-Rapin
Trina Dries
Marlene Marshall
Paul Mitchell
Joe Niemiec
Jill Ruesch
Gary Solberg

1999
Dr. James Golden, Pres.
Cindy Alton
Deb Black
Dede Burk
Trina Conner
Leslie Gilbertie

Joe Niemiec
Jill Ruesch
Gary Solberg

2000
Dr. James Golden, Pres.
Cindy Alton
Deb Black
Dede Burk
Trina Conner
Leslie Covington
Leslie Gilbertie
Joe Niemiec
Jill Ruesch
Gary Solberg

2001
Dr. James Golden, Pres.
Deb Black
Leslie Covington
Mike Foerster
Leslie Gilbertie
Hazel Matlin
Larry Moore
Helen Peterson
Roy Woolfstead

2002
Dr. James Golden, Pres.
Leslie Covington
Yvonne Day
Leslie Gilbertie
Hazel Matlin
Larry Moore
Helen Peterson
Sandra Relyea
Roy Woolfstead

2003
Dr. Andrea Golden, Pres.
Nancy Bosley
Joey Carroll
Yvonne Day
Melissa Harris
Hazel Matlin
Helen Peterson
Sandra Relyea
Diana Woolfstead

2004
Dr. Andrea Golden, Pres.
Charlie Born
Nancy Bosley
Yvonne Day
Melissa Harris
Jim Nelson
Jim Pernell
Lorre Rizzi
Diana Woolfstead

2005
Dr. Andrea Asebedo, Pres.
Kathleen Breslin
Linda Covich
Melissa Harris
Jennifer Kirkland
Jim Nelson
Jim Pernell
Lorre Rizzi
Diana Woolfstead

2006
Dr. Andrea Asebedo, Pres.
Deb Black
Charlie Born
Ace Clemens

Linda Covich
Jennifer Kirkland
Sherry Miller
Jim Pernell
Lorre Rizzi

2007
Dr. Andrea Asebedo, Pres.
Deb Black
Pegi Bockrath
Charlie Born
Ace Clemens
Linda Covich
David Forseth
Jennifer Kirkland
Sherry Miller

2008
Dr. Andrea Asebedo, Pres.
Pegi Bockrath
Jill-Armanda Boland
Charlie Born
Ace Clemens
David Forseth
Doug Hoerber
Sherry Miller
Roy Woolfstead

2009
Rev. Bob Luckin, Pres.
Linda Aldrich
Pegi Bockrath
Jill Boland
Charlie Born
Ace Clemens
Doug Hoerber
Cher Matthews
Tara Steele

2010
Rev. Judith Churchman,
Pres.
Diana Bordeaux
Mike Forester
Dave Forseth
Roger Gray
Doug Hoerber
Jennifer Kirkland
Tara Steele
Gillian Trumbull

2011
Rev. Bob Luckin, Pres.
Sandy Babcock
Diana Bordeaux
Fred Erickson
Kurt Mitchell
Tara Steele
Wendi Stewart
Gillian Trumbull
Diana Woolfstead

2012
Rev. Bob Luckin, Pres.
Sandy Babcock
Pam Brady-White
Fred Erickson
Cher Matthews
Kurt Mitchell
Gene Rand
Gillian Trumbull
Diana Woolfstead

2013
Rev. Mary Mitchell, Pres.
Charlie Born
Fred Erickson

Sally Foster
Carolyn Pearson
Tara Steele
Rev. Kay Stewart
Gillian Trumbull
Diana Woolfstead

2014
Rev. Mary Mitchell, Pres.
Replaced in April by
Rev. David Robinson, Pres.
Jill Boland
Charlie Born
Michael Bordeaux
Pegi Codramac
Sally Foster
Carolyn Pearson
Kelly Rizzi
Rev. Kay Stewart

## Ministers and Practitioners by Year (after vote at Congregational Meeting)

**1980**
Pastor:   Dr. Stephen Zukor
Licensed Practitioners:
    Eddie Magill
    Harry Magill

**1981**
Pastor: Rev. Wilma Burtsell
Licensed Practitioners:
    Pat Gage
    Linda Long

**1987**
Pastor: Rev. James Golden
Licensed Practitioners:
    Pat Gage
    Andrea Golden
    Dorris Payne
    Billie White
Intern Practitioners:
    Chuck Hancock
    Julia Houser
    Marie Newman
    Lisa Whipp

**1988**
Pastor: Rev. James Golden
Licensed Practitioners:
    Pat Gage
    Andrea Golden
    Dorothy Roat
    Billie White
Intern Practitioners:
    Chuck Hancock

Julia Houser
Marie Newman

**1989**
Co-Pastors: Rev. James Golden
and Rev. Andrea Golden
Licensed Practitioners:
    Pat Gage
    Dorothy Roat
Intern Practitioner
    Alta Hancock
    Chuck Hancock
    Marie Newman

**1990**
Co-Pastor: Rev. James Golden
and Rev. Andrea Golden
Licensed Practitioners:
    Dorothy Roat
    Jaine Ryder-Howard
Intern Practitioners:
    Baron Galocy
    Jim Gilbertie,
    Leslie Gilbertie
    Chris Johnson
    Michelle Johnson
    Karen Reidt
    Pam Sanchez
    Toni Thomas
    Kathy Wurm

**1992**
Co-Pastors: Rev. James Golden
and Rev. Andrea Golden
Licensed Practitioners:
    Leslie Gilbertie
    Sandra Lee Rudh
    Jaine Ryder-Howard

Intern Practitioners:
  Karen Grabenstatter
  Chris Johnon
  Michelle Johnson
  Jeffrey Proctor
  Pam Sanchez

### 1993

Co-Pastors: Rev. James Golden
and Rev. Andrea Golden
Staff: Rev. Jaine Ryder-Howard
Licensed Practitioners:
  Leslie Gilbertie
  Karen Grabenstatter
  Sandra Rudh
  Pam Sanchez
Intern Practitioners:
  Carol Chase-Rapin
  Chris Johnson
  Michelle Johnson
  Holly Moore
  Mary Schroeder
  Joanne Shuffelberger
  Toni Thomas

### 1994

Co-Pastors: Dr. James Golden
and Rev. Andrea Golden
Staff:   Rev. Jaine
Ryder-Howard
Licensed Practitioners:
  Leslie Gilbertie
  Pam Sanchez
  Mary Schroeder
Intern Practitioners:
  Carol Chase-Rapin
  Holly Moore
  Joanne Shuffelberger

Toni Thomas

### 1995

Co-Pastors: Dr. James Golden
and Rev. Andrea Golden
Staff:   Rev. Jaine
Ryder-Howard
Licensed Practitioners:
  Holly Moore
  Mary Schroeder
  Joanne Shuffelberger
  Toni Thomas
Intern Practitioners:
Alice Carpenter
  Sharon Kennedy
  Susana Luzier
  Paul Mitchell
  Kay Stewart
  Tresha Wing

### 1996

Co-Pastors: Dr. James Golden
and Rev. Andrea Golden
Licensed Practitioners:
  Carol Chase-Rapin
  Leslie Gilbertie
  Holly Moore
  Pam Sanchez
  Mary Schroeder
  Joanne Shuffelberger
  Toni Thomas-Niemiec
Intern Practitioners:
  Alice Carpenter
  JD Hunt
  Susana Luzier
  Paul Mitchell
  Kay Stewart
  Tresha Wing

1997
Co-Pastors: Dr. James Golden
and Rev. Andrea Golden
Licensed Practitioners:
Alice Carpenter
Carol Chase-Rapin
Leslie Gilbertie
Paul Mitchell
Holly Moore
Pam Sanchez
Mary Schroeder
Joanne Shuffelberger,
Kay Stewart
Toni Thomas-Niemiec
Tresha Wing
Intern Practitioners:
Janet Chenlee
Pegi Codromac
JD Hunt
Teresa Lavagnino
Marleen Marshall
Sue Miller
Joe Niemiec
Christian Rizzi
Jill Ruesch
Kristie Shaw
Nadeen Williams

1998
Co-Pastors: Dr. James Golden
and Rev. Andrea Golden
Assistant: Rev. Carol
Chase-Rapin
Licensed Practitioners:
Alice Carpenter
Leslie Gilbertie
Paul Mitchell
Mary Schroeder

Toni Thomas-Niemiec
Intern Practitioners:
Janet Chenlee
Sharon Kennedy
Teresa Lavagnino
Sue Miller
Joe Niemiec
Nadeen Williams

1999
Co-Pastors: Dr. James Golden
and Dr. Andrea Golden
Assistant: Rev. Carol Chase
Staff:    Rev. Alice Carpenter
Licensed Practitioners:
Leslie Gilbertie
Teresa Lavagnino
Paul Mitchell
Mary Schroeder
Toni Thomas-Niemiec
Intern Practitioners:
Janet Chenlee
Lynn Fritz
Sharon Kennedy
Sue Miller
Joe Niemiec
Darrel Rawlings

2000
Co-Pastors: Dr. James Golden
and Dr. Andrea Golden
Assistant: Rev. Alice Carpenter
Chaplain: Rev. Pam Sanchez
Licensed Practitioners:
Leslie Gilbertie
Teresa Lavagnino
Paul Mitchell
Mary Schroeder

Toni Thomas-Niemiec
Intern Practitioner:
    Lynn Fritz
    Sharon Kennedy
    Sue Miller
    Joe Niemiec
    Darrel Rawlings

## 2001
Co-Pastors: Dr. James Golden
and Dr. Andrea Golden
Staff:   Rev. Alice Carpenter
Chaplain: Rev. Pam Sanchez
Licensed Practitioners:
    Leslie Gilbertie
    Teresa Lavagnino
    Sue Miller
    Mary Schroeder
    Toni Thomas-Niemiec
Intern Practitioners:
    Lynn Fritz
    Sharon Kennedy
    Joe Niemiec
    Darrel Rawlings

## 2002
Co-Pastors: Dr. James Golden
and Dr. Andrea Golden
Staff:   Rev. Toni Niemiec
Chaplain: Rev. Pam Sanchez
Chaplain: Rev. Leslie Gilbertie
Chaplain: Rev. Mary Schroeder
Licensed Practitioners:
    Teresa Lavagnino
    Sue Miller
Intern Practitioners:
    Yvonne Day
    Lynn Fritz

Sharon Kennedy
Barbara Lilly
Joe Niemiec
Darrel Rawlings
Sandra Relyea
Lorre Rizzi

## 2003
Pastor:  Dr. Andrea Golden
Assistant: Rev. Toni Niemiec
Staff:   Rev. Pam Sanchez
         Rev. Mary Schroeder
Licensed Practitioners:
    Yvonne Day
    Sharon Kennedy
    Dana Farrington
    Lynn Fritz
    Teresa Lavagnino
    Barbara Lilley
    Diane Messing
    Sue Miller
    Joe Niemiec
    Sandra Relyea
Intern Practitioners:
    Ace Clemens
    Darrel Rawlings

## 2004
Pastor:  Dr. Andrea Golden
Assistant: Rev. Toni Niemiec
Chaplain: Rev. Pam Sanchez
Staff:   Rev. Mary Schroeder
         Rev. Yvonne Day
         Rev. Lynn Fritz
         Rev. Sharon Kennedy
         Rev. Sue MillerBorn
         Rev. Joe Niemiec
Licensed Practitioners:

Ace Clemens
Dana Farrington
Sally Foster
Barbara Lilley
Intern Practitioners:
Pegi Codromac
Jeannie Fox
Valery Thompson
Sara Woeck-Chulufas

2005
Pastor: Dr. Andrea Asebedo
Assistant: Rev. Toni Niemiec,
Staff: Rev. Yvonne Day
Rev. Lynn Fritz
Rev. Sharon Kennedy
Rev. Sue MillerBorn
Rev. Joe Niemiec
Rev. Pam Sanchez
Rev. Mary Schroeder
Licensed Practitioner:
Ace Clemens
Intern Practitioners:
Pegi Codramac
Valery Thompson

2006
Pastor: Dr. Andrea Asebedo
Assistant: Rev. Toni Niemiec
Staff: Rev. Lynn E. Fritz
Rev. Sue Miller-Born
Rev. Mary Schroeder
Rev. Joe Niemiec
Rev. Pam Sanchez
Licensed Practitioner:
Ace Clemens
Intern Practitioners:
Tienne Beaulieu

Pegi Bockrath
Charlie Born
Ed Brewer
Mark Hoskins
Tim Kersten
Christian Rizzi
Valery Thompson

2007
Pastor: Dr. Andrea Asebedo
Assistant: Rev. Sue MillerBorn,
Staff: Rev. Lynn E. Fritz,
Rev. Sharon Kennedy
Rev. Mary Mitchell
Rev. Pam Sanchez
Licensed Practitioners:
Tienne Beaulieu
Ace Clemens
Intern Practitioners:
Ed Brewer
Mark Hoskins
Christian Rizzi
Valery Thompson

2008
Co-Pastors: Rev. Judith
Churchman and Rev. Bub
Luckin
Minister Emeritus: Dr. Andrea
Asebedo
Staff: Rev. Lynn E. Fritz,
Rev. Sharon Kennedy
Rev. Sue MillerBorn
Rev. Mary Mitchell
Rev. Pam Sanchez
Licensed Practitioners:
Tienne Beaulieu
Ace Clemens

Valery Thompson
Intern Practitioner:
    Ed Brewer

**2009**
Co-Pastors: Rev. Judith
Churchman and Rev. Bob
Luckin
Minister Emeritus: Dr. Andrea
Asebedo
Staff:    Rev. Lynn Fritz,
    Rev. Sharon Kennedy
    Rev. Sue MillerBorn
    Rev. Mary Mitchell
    Rev. Pam Sanchez
Licensed Practitioners:
    Ace Clemens
    Valery Thompson
Intern Practitioners:
    Diana Bordeaux
    Ed Brewer

**2010**
Co-Pastors: Rev. Judith
Churchman and Rev. Bob
Luckin
Minister Emeritus: Dr. Andrea
Asebedo
Assistant: Rev. Sue MillerBorn
    Rev. Mary Mitchell
Staff:    Rev. Sharon Kennedy
    Rev. Pam Sanchez
Licensed Practitioners:
    Tienne Beaulieu
    Ace Clemens
Intern Practitioners:
    Ed Brewer
    Vicky Egar-Klein

Ann Levings
Marylin Miller
Tara Steele

**2011**
Co-Pastors: Rev. Judith
Churchman and Rev. Bob
Luckin
Assistant: Rev. Sue MillerBorn
    Rev. Mary Mitchell
Staff:    Rev. Sharon Kennedy
    Rev. Pam Sanchez
    Rev. Kay Stewart
Licensed Practitioners:
    Tienne Beaulieu
    Ace Clemens
Intern Practitioners:
    Ed Brewer
    Marylin Miller
    Tara Steele

**2012**
Interim Co-Pastors: Rev. Sue
MillerBorn and Rev. Mary
Mitchell
    Rev. Sharon Kennedy
    Rev. Pam Sanchez
    Rev. Kay Stewart
Licensed Practitioners:
    Tienne Beaulieu
    Marylin Miller
    Tara Steele
Intern Practitioners:
    Charlie Born
    Bonnie Metcalf
    Amy Silberstein
    Darcia Slape
    Katie Watters

2013
Interim Co-Pastors: Rev. Sue
MillerBorn and Rev. Mary
Mitchell
Staff:    Rev. Sharon Kennedy
          Rev. Pam Sanchez
          Rev. Kay Stewart
Affiliated: Rev. Barbara Leger
Licensed Practitioners:
          Charlie Born
          Marylin Miller
          Tara Steele

Intern Practitioners:
          Diana Johnson
          Bonnie Metcalf
          Amy Silberstein
          Katie Watters

2014
Pastor (as of 4/7) Rev. David
Robinson
Assistant: Rev. Sue MillerBorn
          Rev. Mary Mitchell
Staff:    Rev. Sharon Kennedy
          Rev. Pam Sanchez
          Rev. Kay Stewart
Affiliated: Rev. Barbara Leger
Licensed Practitioners:
          Charlie Born
          Diana Johnson
          Marylin Miller
Intern Practitioner:
          Bonnie Metcalf

## December 1979 Redding Science of Mind Center Members

*Underlined names are those currently members of CSL Redding in 2014.*

Abbott, C. R.
Adams, Carol
Alsop, Joan
Anderson, Arnold
Anderson, Lynette
Arendall, Colleen
Baril, June Ann
Barnes, Margaret
Bell, Katherine
Benedict, Trudy
Benner, Marge
Biggerstaff, Edith
Bobich, Carol
Bobich, John
Bobich, Wilda
Borg, Tarquin
Bruno, John
Branch, Vivian
Butler, Kassey
Butler, Mary Ellen
Calloway, Mildred
Calvert, Lea
Carden,Timothy
Carrico, Janiece
Childs, Max
Childs, Pat
Cantin, Marilyn
Craver, Corienne
Chapman, Marvin
Churchill, Ann

Churchill, Don
Clark, Dorothy
Coleman, Lew
Cook, Phyllis
Cos, Florence
Cox, William
Culhane, Benda
Davis, Miles
Dean, Echo
Dickson, Jeffrey
Dinsdale, William
Drummond, Jan
Dethlefs, Billie Sue
Ducklow, Elaine
Duncan, Betty
Duncan, Bart
Ellis, Katheryn
Elliston, Ruth
Emmsley, Elizabeth
Erickson, Fred
Erickson, Patty
Edwards, Bobbie
Edwards, John
Erickson, John Raymond
Evans, Clem
Evans, Margaret
Evans, Marilyn
Eqing, Barbara
Ewing, Ed
Feusi, Adolph
Fowler, Floyd
Gage, Patricia
Gardon, Ruby
Gifford, Jan
Guy, Dorothy
Guy, Kenneth
Haley, Jean
Haley, Jim

Herrin, Jack

Herrin, Marlene

Holly, Alice

Holly, Robert

Huebner, Barbara

Huntoon, Dorothy

Huntoon, Robert

Hurley, Jere

Hylton, Emily

Innis, Dorothy

Jahnke, Margaret

Jensen, Howard

Jensen, Lillian

Johnson, Bruce

Johnson, Dorothy

Kay, Heather

Kachele, Dorothy

Keith, Marie

Kendeigh, Dorothy

Knighten, Jean

LaMour, Hal

LaMour, Paulette

Latiolais, Mardell

Lee, Pam

Lonas, Fred

Lonas, Trammell

Long, Frank

Long, Linda

Lyon, Patricia

Madden, Vera

Mosher, Ross

Magill, Edwin

Hagill, Harry

Mann, Florence

Maxwell, Chris

Maxwell, Mike

McDaniel, Alberta

McDaniel, Elizabeth

McDaniel, Gary

McKeown, Priscilla

McLaughlin, Sandi

McComb, Fletcher

McComb, Virginia

Moore, Bob

Moore, Dorothy

Moore, William

Morris, Nancy

Moses, Sandi

Milbrandt, Lizzie

Miller, Rynd

Munson, Jessie

Noble, Dean

Nutter, Betty

Oddon, Carolyn

Owens, Audrey Irene

Peet, Dorothy

Peet, Hank

Pence, Erin

Phillips, Edna

Phillips, Leslie

Pratt, Jana

Pursell, Jenny

Pyshora, Marlene

Qualls, Ruby

Ray, Kacey

Richmond, Daisy

Richmond, Jim

Roberts, Bill

Roth, Carl

Roth, Marcella

Rittenhouse, Irene

Rittenhouse, Joseph

Rodgers, Hazel

Ryan, Judith

Salidbury, Melva

Sateren, Al

Schell, Ethelene
Scarbrough, Alice
Seiffert, Peggy
Seiffert, William
Shearer, Bill
Shearer, Sue
Stevens, Genevieve
Thomas, Pam
Todt, Vickie
Trotta, Frank
Taff, Janice
Vanick, Helen
Voitich, Lydia
Walker, David
Walker, Margaret
Waterhouse, David
Waterhouse, Melva
Willis, Donna
Willis, Phillip
Whetstone, Carole
Whetstone, Larry
Wise, Al
Wittner, Candace
Wootton, Hal
Wootton, Marian
Wright, Heston
Wright, Marjorie
Yarbrough, Patricia
Yerves, Dorothy
Zukor, Dr. Stephen
Zuza, Phillis

# PERMISSIONS RECEIVED

**From the Redding Record Searchlight Newspaper**

| Date of Article | Article Headline |
| --- | --- |
| 5/9/1977 | Seeing oneness with the creator |
| April 1977 | Science of Mind goals are right thinking, action. |
| 7/1/1978 | Science of Mind: We are all co-creators with God. |
| 8/23/1980 | Faith emphasizes mind power |
| 9/19/1981 | New minister of the Redding Science of Mind Center is Rev. James Golden |
| 5/7/1983 | There's Science to faith |
| 6/13/1993 | Golden rule: Couple follows spiritual path. |

| Other Photos: | Images |
| --- | --- |
| D. Andrea (Golden) Asebedo | 7c, 12a, 13, 14, 20, 22, 23, 25, |
| Dr. James Golden | 4, 7c, 11, 13, 14, 19, 20 |
| Sherry Miller | 5, 12a |
| Rev. Sue MillerBorn | 6a, 29a |
| Rev. Mary Mitchell | 12a, 20, 29b |
| Rev. David Robinson | 31 |
| Rev. Judith Churchman | 27 |
| Rev. Bob Luckin | 27 |
| Chris Johnson | 6c |
| Christian Rizzi | 18c |
| Brad Fay | 20 |

| | |
|---|---|
| Joanne Fay | 20 |
| Jaine Ryder | 20 |
| Teresa Lavanino | 20 |
| Paul Mitchell | 20 |
| Sandra Relyea | 22 |
| Lorie Rizzi | 22 |
| Kathy Hooykiss | 22 |
| Harry Bleile | 24 |

# ABOUT THE AUTHOR

Rev. Mary Mitchell has been a member of the Center for Spiritual Living, Redding since 1989. Her passion for writing led her to interview many of the original members of the Center in the early 1990s and save many of the historical documents used to create this manuscript. She received her practitioner license in 1993, minister license in 2003, and was ordained in 2008. Rev. Mary and Rev. Sue MillerBorn served as interim co-pastors during the Center's search for a new senior minister, who was hired in April 2014. Rev. Mary and Rev. Sue now both happily serve the Center as Assistant Ministers.